Mexican Slow Cooker Cookbook

Mexican Slow Cooker Cookbook

*Easy, Flavorful Mexican Dishes
That Cook Themselves*

Marye Audet

**ROCKRIDGE
PRESS**

This book is dedicated to the readers of Restless Chipotle,
who encourage me daily, and help me test and perfect recipes.

CONTENTS

INTRODUCTION

There is a warm richness and unique flavor to Mexican food that is unmistakable, and much of that comes from a long tradition of low and slow cooking. For hundreds of years—perhaps even thousands—Mexican chefs and home cooks have passed recipes from generation to generation. And in many Mexican kitchens, a simple earthenware or metal pot called an *olla* (or *cazuela*) bubbles on the stove all day long, melding complex flavors in sauces, plumping dried beans, or slowly transforming tough meats into buttery-soft shreds.

If you have neither the time to spend slaving over the stove all day nor an *abuela* (grandmother) who can do it for you, the idea of creating tender and tasty Mexican food at home can seem pretty impossible. Luckily, just about every traditional Mexican recipe that requires long hours of cooking can be reimagined in the slow cooker. This modern appliance is perfect for simmering meats and gives sauces time to develop the warm and deep complexity that makes Mexican food beloved by so many. And there's no stirring required, so you can put everything in the cooker in the morning, turn it on, and come home at the day's end to a finished meal.

In this book you'll find more than 80 slow cooker recipes for everything from Mexican and Mexican-inspired appetizers to desserts. Each has been adapted to be made easily, to require little preparation time, and to work perfectly in your slow cooker. You'll learn how to use this handy appliance to its full potential and become familiar with the tools and ingredients you'll need to prepare Mexican food, from authentic dishes to popular, if less traditional, restaurant fare, almost effortlessly.

Chapters 1 and 2 walk you through the basics of slow cooking, as preparing for and getting the most out of popular ingredients in Mexican cooking. You may be tempted to skim over this part and head straight to the recipes if you have plenty of cooking experience. However, it's important that you give it a read because these chapters lay the foundation that you'll need to complete the recipes successfully. There are techniques, tricks, and tips for using ingredients in both traditional and nontraditional ways to achieve the flavors of Mexico at home.

In the rest of the book you'll find a range of recipes, along with hints and suggestions on how to select or substitute ingredients, reduce or raise the heat of a dish, and much more.

¡Adelante! Let's go!

1

SLOW COOKING 101

~~~~~~~~~~~~~~~~~~~~~

Slow cookers work the same way whether you are cooking French, Mexican, or plain old American dishes. Once you are familiar with how these appliances work and how to use them most efficiently, you will be well on your way to slow cooking–expert status.

Many of the new models of slow cookers have programmable touch pads, built-in meat thermometers, and other accessories to make your cooking chores even easier. They can be programmed for how many hours you want cooking to last, and then, after those hours are up, many modern slow cookers will switch automatically to warm, keeping the food at the proper temperature until you are ready to eat. Not all makes and models have these features, so if you are planning to purchase a new slow cooker, your first step should be comparing the various models and brands.

THE BENEFITS OF SLOW COOKING

There are a variety of reasons to have a slow cooker among your appliances. Here are some of the benefits of this handy kitchen helper:

Slow cookers are convenient. A slow cooker allows you to toss some ingredients into a pot in the morning, set the heat, and walk out the door. When you get home, tired after a long day of work and errands, your dinner is ready and waiting to be served. There aren't a lot of pans and dishes to clean up, either.

Slow cooking enhances flavor development. Long, slow cooking allows flavors to develop to their fullest, richest, and most delicious. Many ingredients, tomatoes, for example, do not benefit from being cooked at high temperatures. A slow cooker gently coaxes every bit of flavor from each ingredient without the bitterness that sometimes occurs when foods are cooked at too high a temperature.

Slow cooker ingredients are budget friendly. Cooking large cuts of meat in a slow cooker gives the meat a chance to break down and become tender. It's an excellent choice for cooking chuck roasts and other tough cuts of meat that are less expensive than tenderloin or ribeye steaks.

Slow-cooked food doesn't burn. It's pretty easy to get distracted by children, phone calls, or the doorbell when you are cooking. You may end up returning to the kitchen to find that dinner is way beyond caramelized. That won't happen when you're using a slow cooker. The temperature is low enough that food generally doesn't scorch, burn, or stick to the bottom, even if you get called away for an extended period of time.

SLOW COOKER BASICS

Using a slow cooker is not rocket science, but there are a few things you should know to get the most out of it:

Keep an eye on it—just once. If you've never used your slow cooker before, make sure you are at home when you use it for the first time. Different brands may vary in temperature, and there is always a chance that the appliance is not calibrated right. Observing it cooking on each setting can help avoid problems such as over- or undercooking.

ON CROCK-POTS AND SLOW COOKERS

What's the difference between a Crock-Pot and a slow cooker? Crock-Pot is the registered trademark of Rival Company, which released the slow cooker in 1970. So while every Crock-Pot is a slow cooker, not every slow cooker is a Crock-Pot. Crock-Pots have heating elements on the bottom and sides, but slow cookers usually have them only on the bottom. Many people use the word "Crock-Pot" instead of slow cooker, and the two words have come to have the same meaning. This book sticks to the words "slow cooker," but the recipes will work in any slow cooker or Crock-Pot.

Keep a lid on it. Taking the lid off of your slow cooker while your food is cooking releases valuable heat and can significantly slow down your cooking time. In fact, you'll have to add 15 to 30 minutes of cooking time each time the lid is removed. Most cookers have transparent lids so you can see what is going on in the cooker. Don't take the top off until about 30 minutes before you expect your dish to be finished. You can check doneness then.

Thaw frozen foods. Do not put frozen foods in the slow cooker without thawing them first. The combination of the frozen food and the heating element under the crock can cause it to crack. Not only does it ruin your dinner, but it also makes a huge mess. The exceptions to this are the slow cooker dinners in the freezer section of the grocery store. Follow the instructions on the package.

Take care of the crock. The crock—the crockery insert inside of the slow cooker—can break, crack, or chip. Always hand wash it and dry it with a soft cloth. When you take the crock out of the heating part, don't put it on a granite or marble counter or any other cold surface. Place it on a folded towel instead, and you won't have to worry about it cracking.

Adapt for high-altitude cooking. If you live at a higher altitude, you'll need to add 30 minutes of cooking time for each hour specified in the recipe. If your recipe instructs you to cook the dish for 8 hours, you'll need to add 4 hours for a total of 12 hours.

Don't store food in the crock. Since the crock is made to hold heat for a long period of time, food should not be stored in it. It won't cool down fast enough to prevent the growth of harmful bacteria, and the food won't be safe to eat. Just transfer the food to a tightly sealed container.

FREEZING SLOW-COOKED FOODS

Many of the recipes in this book will generate more food than you can eat in one meal. Freezing leftovers in a zippered freezer bag or freezer container is a great option for continuing to enjoy the work your slow cooker did for you. And by freezing leftovers in single-serving sizes, any family member can have a grab-and-go meal in minutes. The question is, which Mexican foods freeze well and which don't?

As a general rule, do not freeze:

- **homemade, cream-based sauces**, which will often separate

- **cooked rice**, because it will get mushy

- **diced potatoes**, which take on an unappetizing texture once frozen. Mashed potatoes, however, can be frozen, thawed, and reheated without issue.

The foods you do freeze should generally be eaten within three months of freezing.

Before freezing, make sure the leftovers have cooled to room temperature. It's then safe to cover tightly before freezing in a casserole dish, zippered freezer bag, or individual-serving-size bag. When you're ready to reheat the meal, just remove it from the freezer and let it thaw overnight in the refrigerator. You can heat it the next day in an oven preheated to 375°F. Allow it to bake uncovered for about 20 minutes. If you forget to thaw in advance, you can bake the leftovers, covered, for one hour at 375°F, or until heated through. Remove the cover for the last 15 minutes of cooking.

Having a couple of meals cooked and frozen is a great stress reliever during those busy times of the year. You know the ones: January through December.

KNOW YOUR SLOW COOKER

The more you understand about how a slow cooker works, the easier it will be for you to use it successfully. You'll find cookers in several sizes, ranging from a tiny ½-quart model to a substantial 8-quart size. The one you choose will depend on the size of your family and what you intend to cook. Given how relatively inexpensive most slow cookers are, you might even want to consider purchasing more than one.

Size
The smallest slow cookers you should consider range from 1½- to 2-quart round slow cookers. They are ideal for single people and couples with no children. But even if you're cooking for a family, it's nice to have a small slow cooker to use for making dips and sauces. In chapter 3 you will find recipes for appetizers, dips, and sauces.

Larger-sized slow cookers are better for families of four or more who like to cook once and enjoy multiple meals from that effort. Most of the recipes in this book are ideal for a 5-quart cooker. This size is good for families of four or five that like to have leftovers to use for another meal. This size also works well for people who entertain.

Shape

Before you buy, consider how you'll be using your cooker. Round cookers are perfect for soups or stews, and large oval cookers are best for roasts and whole cuts of meat. The oval is the more versatile of the two shapes.

Temperature Range

Most slow cookers have low and high settings. Some also have a warm setting that is automatically turned on when the cooking time is finished. This feature is more than just a convenience—it ensures that your food will be held at a safe temperature until you are back home and ready to eat.

The low cooking temperature is usually 170°F, and the high cooking temperature is usually 200°F, but these temperatures vary from manufacturer to manufacturer. Whenever possible, the recipes in this book give you cooking times for both settings. Generally speaking, you'll get a more flavorful, tender dish on the lower setting, but there will be times when you don't mind sacrificing a little quality so you can have it on the table sooner.

USING YOUR SLOW COOKER: DOS AND DON'TS

Now that you have the basics under your belt, here are a few essential dos and don'ts of slow cooking. Always read through the user's manual to get specific instructions on how to care for your appliance.

DO spray the insert of your slow cooker with cooking spray or use a disposable liner before cooking. There are a couple of reasons for this. First of all, it makes for much easier cleanup, but the most important reason is that it protects the glaze of the crockery insert. When food sticks, the process of scraping it off of the crockery can damage and remove the glaze. If you're making a soup or a dish with lots of sauce, it's not necessary to spray the crock.

DO use fresh, high-quality ingredients. How many times have you heard the statement that your dish is only as good as the ingredients that go into it? This is especially true with slow cooking because an ingredient that is slightly off can give a bad flavor to the other ingredients in the cooker. For the most flavor and best results, your ingredients should be as fresh as possible, without bruises, withering, or soft spots.

DO cut ingredients into consistent sizes so everything cooks at the same rate.
If ingredients are cut in random sizes, you may end up with some that are cooked
and some that are raw. Consistency in preparation will result in a perfectly cooked
meal. Also guard against cutting foods too small. Unless your recipe states otherwise, vegetables should be added whole or in chunks rather than chopped or diced.
If they are too small, they'll cook down and disappear into the sauce during the long
cooking time.

DO prepare meat properly before putting it in a slow cooker. Always remove
excess fat from the meat. The fat will break down over the long cooking time and
collect in the sauce, making it look and feel greasy. Take the skin off poultry as well.
The skin will not get crispy but will become limp and rubbery in the moist heat.

DO layer ingredients in the proper order. Firm vegetables like potatoes, carrots,
onions, and so on should be placed on the bottom of the slow cooker. Put meats
on top of the firm vegetables, and then layer in tender vegetables like corn, mushrooms, and spinach or hold them out of the slow cooker until the last 30 minutes of
cooking time. Add dried herbs and spices at the beginning of the cooking time. Add
fresh herbs at the end unless the recipe directs you to add them first.

DON'T use your slow cooker near an open window or air conditioner vent. The
draft and cooler air can keep it from heating properly. Your slow cooker works by
cooking with slow, even heat. It may not seem as if the breeze from a fan is a big
deal, but it can cool off the top enough to keep your recipe from cooking properly
and even slow down cooking time.

DON'T use your slow cooker to reheat foods. Slow cookers can't heat foods up to
a safe temperature fast enough. If you try to reheat foods in your slow cooker, they

HOW TO ADJUST RECIPES FOR YOUR SLOW COOKER

You can adjust recipe yields up or down as
long as the slow cooker is never less than half
or more than two-thirds full; lower-yield recipes will take 6 to 8 hours on low heat to cook,
and higher-yield recipes will take 8 to 10 hours
on low heat to cook. If you're in a pinch, you
can make any dish in half the time by increas-
ing the cooking temperature, but be prepared
for there to be flavor and texture differences
in the final product. The general rule for
adjusting the temperature in a recipe is that
1 hour on high is equal to 2 hours on low.

could become contaminated with harmful bacteria, causing salmonella or other food-borne illnesses. Remove leftovers from the slow cooker when you are done cooking and store them in another airtight container in the fridge. When you are ready to reheat them, do so on top of the stove or in the microwave.

DON'T add too much liquid. Foods release liquid during cooking, and since the cooker is covered, the liquids condense on the lid and drip back down into the pot. If you do happen to end up with too much liquid, take the lid off and cook uncovered for 30 minutes.

DON'T use the full amount of wine called for if you are adapting a recipe from the stove-top version. The alcohol does not evaporate as much in a slow cooker as it does in the oven or on top of the stove, so you could end up with a strong alcohol flavor and tipsy dinner guests. It's fine to use the full amount called for in a slow cooker recipe since the author has already adapted it.

DON'T turn the slow cooker off before the end of the cooking time. While heat will remain for some time, there is no way to control it or to be sure that your dinner is at a safe temperature. In the same way, if your electricity goes off for more than 10 or 15 minutes during cooking, don't try to save the meal. Throw it out and head to the nearest *taqueria*.

2

EVERYDAY MEXICAN SLOW COOKING

~~~~~~~~~~~~~~~~~~~~~

While it may seem daunting to prepare Mexican food at home, there's no reason you should reserve these meals only for special occasions or long, lazy weekends. With the right planning, you can overcome the issue of time and return home to the soothing, spicy aroma of *pozole* or tender *barbacoa* any night of the week. Use your days off to make sauces and chop ingredients, or, if you're really in a pinch, purchase commercially prepared sauces at the grocery store—some are healthier than others, and some are more flavorful than others. Try several kinds until you find what you like best.

FLAVORFUL MEXICAN COOKING AT ITS BEST

The recipes included in this book are adapted to require as little prep time as possible yet maintain those mouthwatering flavors of Mexico. You'll find some recipes that have a "Quick Prep" icon. This signifies that there is almost no prep time at all, perhaps just chopping an ingredient or two. You can use these recipes when you are in a rush to get out the door. The other recipes are formulated to take 20 minutes or less to put together, and you can do the prep work either in the morning or the night before. Because the morning is a busy time for most households, it's often more convenient to prep a few items in the evening.

Many Mexican dishes are soups or stews that require long simmering to bring out all the flavors of the ingredients. There is no better way to create them than by putting them in the slow cooker in the morning and ladling fragrant spoonfuls of tender meat onto the family's plates in the evening. And since everything cooks in one dish, cleanup is a breeze.

Possibly the best thing of all about a slow cooker is that you can cook meals in the summer without heating up the kitchen. When it's so hot that the frosting melts right off your cupcakes and the air conditioner is working overtime, the slow cooker allows you to head for the coolest room in the house with a glass of *horchata* and a good book.

BELOVED MEXICAN FOODS

Almost everyone has a craving for Mexican food once in a while. You might go to a big chain restaurant, a little mom-and-pop place, or a Mexican fast-food joint, but regardless of where you go to satisfy the craving, the desire is very real.

The real dishes and flavors of Mexico vary according to region. In the north, along the border, beef, game, and other meats are popular. With so much coastline, it shouldn't be a surprise that seafood is king in coastal regions like the Baja Peninsula, Sinaloa, and Veracruz. The southern areas of the country—Oaxaca, Puebla, and others—utilize more chicken and a greater variety of vegetables in their recipes. While you may be able to get a taco in any city in Mexico, the ingredients will be different from one place to another.

Many of your favorite Mexican foods can be made and served right from your slow cooker, but others will serve as fillings for tacos and other favorite street foods such as those that follow. The slow-cooker recipes in this book have been written so you do as little work in the kitchen as possible. That said, there are certain items that you can make over the weekend that don't require the slow cooker. You'll find recipes for these more hands-on cooking projects in chapter 10 (see page 143).

SLOW-COOKED MEAT

The long cooking time involved in slow cooking allows you to create budget-friendly meals with inexpensive cuts of meat, such as chuck roasts and flank steaks. As the meat cooks, it absorbs the flavors of the aromatics, vegetables, and other ingredients in the recipe, resulting in a finished dish that provides bite after bite of complex deliciousness. Keep in mind that lean meats can dry out, so adding a little fat, like bacon, will help keep them moist and give them flavor, too. Remember, the slow cooker will do most of the work for you. The indigenous people of Mexico may have had only basic utensils, and they certainly did not have time to waste on food preparation.

ENCHILADAS

The word *enchilada* simply means "in chile." The Mexican version bears little resemblance to the plate full of filled tortillas smothered in sauce that you get at your favorite restaurant. In Mexico, tortillas are dipped into a warm sauce, filled with meat, and quickly rolled up. Although the Aztec living in the lake region in central Mexico were known to roll corn tortillas around small fish on occasion and the early explorer Cortés served them at celebrations, the word "enchilada" did not show up in North America until the late 1800s.

QUESADILLAS

The original quesadillas were flattened pieces of *masa de nixtamal*, a dough made from ground corn kernels that had been soaked in water with slaked lime. They enclosed ingredients such as meat, vegetables, and chiles, and then were cooked on a hot surface. In the sixteenth century, the Aztec empire fell during the Spanish conquest. Historians and other scholars of Latin America have written much on the political, social, and cultural effects of colonization, but for our simpler purposes, it's worth noting that the arrival of the Spanish meant the arrival of cheese as well. The Spanish are the ones who dubbed it "quesadilla," which literally means "little cheesy thing."

TO PREP OR NOT TO PREP?

Are there really benefits to prepping ingredients before putting them in the slow cooker?

Certain types of prep work are essential. For example, vegetables must be chopped in uniform sizes so they cook evenly. However, other types of cooking-related prep can often be sidestepped in the interest of simplicity.

Browning meats gives them a nice color and adds flavor, but it isn't essential if you don't have time to do it. In a similar way, *charring* and *roasting* vegetables can add a subtle smokiness if you have time to do it, but you can skip these kinds of preparation if time is an issue. You will lose some of the nuanced flavors of a more traditional Mexican dish, but for a much shorter prep time and with one less skillet to clean, you'll still come away with a bold and delicious meal.

The traditional quesadilla is a fried or griddled tortilla with mild *queso* (cheese). In the United States, quesadillas are usually made with Monterey Jack or Cheddar cheese melted between two flour tortillas. Many of the Mexican recipes that have become popular in the United States are actually Tex-Mex or Cal-Mex, versions adapted by settlers in the border states of Texas and California.

SALSA

Salsa simply means "sauce." In this book, there are recipes for cooked table salsas and salsas used for cooking. While there are dozens of basic salsas, one of the most basic is a combination of vine-ripened tomatoes, tomatillos, onions, chiles, lime juice, and cilantro, coarsely chopped and sprinkled with a little salt. This version, however, didn't pre-date the Spanish Conquest. The Aztec did not have onions, garlic, lime, or cilantro until after colonization. And the only "true" salsa that has lime juice in it is a salsa Mexicana (commonly known as *pico de gallo*) or a Yucatec *xni pec.*

TACOS

Tacos are classic street food in Mexico. The fillings vary according to the region, but they generally consist of some sort of protein or vegetable in either a crispy or soft tortilla with additions such as lettuce or cabbage, salsa, cheese, and avocados. Tacos' origins are unclear, but the term *taco* is believed to date from eighteenth-century silver mines in Mexico.

TAMALES

Tamales go back almost as far as Mexican history. There is evidence that ancient cooks were making them as early as 2,500 BCE. They consist of masa dough, unfilled or filled with meat, vegetables, chiles, or a combination of ingredients, then wrapped in a leaf or corn husk and steamed or boiled. Tamales are a portable food, so they were commonly eaten by soldiers, hunters, and other travelers. Tamales could be made ahead of time, transported easily, and warmed in the coals of the fire when it was time for dinner.

THE MEXICAN KITCHEN

As with any other cuisine, there are ingredients that are unique and essential to Mexican cooking. The following list is by no means complete, but it does include the ingredients you will use most often for the recipes in this book.

PANTRY

Beans: Pinto beans and black beans are used most often. Buy them in cans free of bisphenol A (BPA), a chemical in the lining of some cans that may harm your health. If a can is BPA-free, it should be labeled as such. Many people choose to soak and cook dried beans in a slow cooker, which does the job marvelously. The only hitch is that you need to plan ahead so you have cooked beans on hand for some of the recipes in this book. If you cook beans from scratch, make a large batch and freeze some of it. You'll then have the beans ready—without the concerns that come with most canned beans—when you need them.

Chicken, beef, and vegetable stocks: Stock is different from broth and has more flavor. You can make your own and keep it on hand—it freezes well. Stock is used as a base for soups and sauces, as well slow-cooked meat.

Chipotle (dried) and chipotles in adobo (canned): Chipotles are simply smoked jalapeños. Dried chipotles can be ground to a powder or reconstituted and made into a paste for use in recipes. Chipotles in adobo are canned chipotles in a smoky red sauce that add heat and flavor to many different dishes. The two can often be used interchangeably.

Rice: Rice, like corn, can be used with beans to create a complete protein. You can use either brown or white medium-grain rice, but do not use instant rice, because the result will be gummy and mushy.

Tomato sauce and paste: Tomato sauce and tomato paste are good to have on hand for making sauces and adding to soups and stews. Keep canned (BPA-free) diced tomatoes in your pantry so you can make salsa in a pinch.

Tortillas: Corn tortillas can be fried and made into taco shells, tostada shells, and chips. They are used for enchiladas and other dishes as well. Flour tortillas are used for dishes like burritos and chimichangas and are sometimes served plain with butter.

PRODUCE

Avocados: Avocados add richness and texture to many foods and are essential for guacamole. Add them to salads and tacos, or top enchiladas with some diced avocado and tomato. Do not keep avocados in the refrigerator.

Cilantro: If you buy only one fresh herb to keep on hand, this should be it. Cilantro gives a fresh, summery taste to recipes. You can add it in the last hour of slow cooking, as well as to garnish your dish once served.

Corn: Often combined with beans to create a complete protein, corn can be served as a side dish, used in stews and soups, or added as a filling for classic Mexican foods like tacos, burritos, and enchiladas. Fresh or frozen corn works equally as well. If you can, buy organic, which is sure to be free of genetically modified organisms (GMOs).

Garlic: Garlic finds its way into many Mexican dishes, such as salsa and enchiladas. Choose plump heads of garlic that don't look dried out. Never use the peeled garlic in jars—it just doesn't have flavor.

Jalapeños: Jalapeños are small chiles that are fairly hot. They are used in many Mexican dishes, and you can always add more or less of them to taste. Remove the seeds if you want to cut back on the amount of heat they add to a dish.

Limes: In Mexico, limes are served with almost everything. A wedge of tangy lime squeezed over your taco brings a bright flavor to the dish. Keep plenty of limes on hand. If your dish seems a little bland, give it a quick squeeze of lime before serving.

Onions: Onions are chopped and used in salsas or blended into sauces. They are essential in meat and poultry stocks and add flavor to nearly every dish you'll cook. Generally, white onions are used in Mexican cooking, but you can use whatever type you like best.

Tomatoes and avocados should not be refrigerated. Keep fresh tomatoes and avocados at room temperature until you've cut into them.

Tomatoes: Tomatoes are used in every way possible in Mexican cooking. Roma tomatoes or other types of plum tomatoes are best for cooking because they are meatier and more flavorful than other tomato varieties when cooked. They should not be kept in the refrigerator.

DAIRY

Cheese: Grated cheese is used in many Mexican dishes. In the United States, it's likely to be Cheddar or Monterey Jack, but in Mexico it's likely to be queso fresco or queso blanco. These cheeses are common in grocery stores in the southwestern United States but may be hard to find elsewhere. You can substitute Cheddar or Jack if you can't find queso.

ALL ABOUT CHILES

Chiles have been an integral part of Mexican food since the Maya first added them to boiling water when making beans. They are responsible for the complexity of many Mexican dishes, and they are often used in dried form as a thickener for sauces.

Roasted chiles are also very common in Mexican cuisine; they are easy to prepare, and they add smoky flavor to any recipe. When you are roasting chiles, keep your face away from any resulting steam and smoke. These contain oils that can irritate your eyes and lungs. Always wear gloves when working with fresh chiles, and keep your hands away from your face.

DRIED CHILES

Drying or dehydrating was one of the first preservation methods ever used in civilization. It ensured that there would be plenty to eat during the winter, but at some point, the Mexican people realized that when chiles were dried, they took on a totally different flavor.

There are hundreds of varieties of dried chiles. Some are well-known, others are regional, and still others are hidden away in small, unknown towns. Don't be afraid to try chiles that are unknown to you and even substitute unfamiliar chiles for those called for in these recipes. Here are some tips for choosing and cooking with dried chiles:

- Choose dried chiles that are not brittle. Brittle chiles are old and might have lost a lot of flavor. When you can, choose chiles that are pliable and soft.

- Store chiles in a cool, dry place.

- Use gloves when working with dried chiles, just as you would when working with fresh ones.

- Much of the heat is in the seeds. When you seed chiles, save the seeds to be added to foods that need a little more heat.

- For more flavor, toast dried chiles in a dry pan or on a comal before using. To do this, after the seeds are removed, open the

TYPES OF CHILES FROM THE MILDEST TO THE HOTTEST

Banana peppers (chiles gueros): These can range from mild to hot and are pale yellow in color.

Pasilla: A dried chile with an earthy flavor and mild spiciness.

Guajillo: A long, pointy dried chile with a maroon color, almost tangy flavor, and mild heat. It is one of the most commonly used chiles in many parts of Mexico.

Jalapeño: One of the most common chiles, this fresh green or red pepper has a rounded point and milder taste than most. Removing the seeds will cut down the heat as well.

Mulato: This dried chile is almost black and has a mild, chocolaty flavor.

chiles up so they are flat and then place them in the preheated pan. Watch them carefully and turn them often. They are done when they just start to have dark spots, after about 30 seconds.

- After they are toasted, soak the chiles in hot but not boiling tap water for 30 minutes. The softened chiles can then be added to recipes as is or puréed, whichever is indicated. Don't pour the cooking water down the drain if you will be puréeing the chiles; instead, use it to thin the purée if necessary, as it holds a lot of the flavor. It can help with consistency of the purée and enhances, rather than dilutes, the flavor.

TO ROAST FRESH CHILES

1. Choose smooth, fresh green or red chiles.

2. Wash and dry the chiles.

3. **To broil:** Preheat the broiler. Place the chiles on a heavy baking sheet under the broiler. Watch carefully, turning every minute, until they blacken. This will take about 5 minutes.

To grill: Preheat the grill. Place the chiles on the grill, turning often, until they are blackened.

To torch: Place the chiles on a heatproof surface and char them with a chef's or plumber's torch, turning them until they are blackened on all sides.

4. When the chiles are charred, remove them from the heat and seal them in a paper bag for about 10 minutes. Take them out and rub off the blackened skin. They are now ready to use.

Poblano: This fresh pepper has a deep green skin and a rich, almost fruity flavor.

Ancho: This is a dried poblano with a beautiful crimson color.

Chipotle: A smoked jalapeño, the chipotle has a rich, smoky flavor and a lot of heat.

Serrano: A small, elongated pepper, the serrano looks similar to a jalapeño but packs a lot more heat.

Habanero: This small pepper comes in red, green, or yellow and is always hot. Habaneros are 30 times hotter than jalapeños.

CHOOSING FRESH, FROZEN, CANNED, OR DRIED

When it comes to selecting ingredients, the choices often include fresh, frozen, canned, and dried options. Canned and dried foods are certainly convenient to have in the pantry. Fresh foods tend to be healthier and have more flavor than canned or dried foods. How can you decide?

Fresh: There is nothing better than fresh, seasonal ingredients. These items offer flavor at its peak. But if you are buying fresh vegetables in the grocery store out of season, they will not be at their best. If they aren't marked organic, they are also likely to have been treated with pesticides. Fortunately for you and your avocado habit (the one you currently have or will develop as your Mexican food consumption increases), avocados are one of the "clean fifteen" fruits and vegetables. That means they are treated with no or low amounts of pesticides. You don't need to buy organic avocados if organic isn't available. On page 161, you can review the other foods on the Clean Fifteen list, as well as the Dirty Dozen fruits and vegetables, which should always be purchased organic since they're treated with high amounts of pesticides in conventional farming.

Frozen: In the winter months, when very few vegetables are in season and the imported options come with hefty price tags, check out the frozen vegetable section in your local grocery store. These vegetables have been blanched and flash-frozen at the peak of ripeness, so they retain most of their nutrients, unlike many imported vegetables that lose more nutrients the longer they travel from farm to market. Look for BPA-free bags or packages emblazoned with the USDA "U.S. Fancy" shield. This shield verifies that the enclosed vegetables are of optimal size, shape, and color and therefore will have better health benefits than lower grades such as "U.S. No. 1" or "U.S. No. 2."

Canned: The lining of cans often contains BPA. Look for processed tomatoes in glass jars or cartons. There are also several organic companies that use BPA-free cans. A quick Internet search should give you a list of them. Canned tomatoes, tomato sauce, and tomato paste are real time-savers.

Dried: Using dried or canned beans can be a tough decision as well. Dried are certainly less expensive, but canned are much more convenient and take very little time to prepare. With canned you'll need to consider the possibility of BPA, too. When it comes to herbs, you also have a choice of fresh or dried. In Mexican cooking you'll want to use both. There is no substitute for fresh cilantro, for example. However, many other herbs are fine to use dry.

ESSENTIAL KITCHEN TOOLS

Although the slow cooker is the appliance you will use the most as you make these recipes, there are other tools that will make your work much easier.

Cast iron griddle or comal (a flat-bottomed cast iron pan): You'll want one of these for roasting peppers, making tortillas, and putting a quick sear on meat. If you don't have a cast iron pan, a heavy stainless steel skillet will do. Do not use a nonstick skillet, since it is not advised for cooking with high heat.

Molcajete: Traditionally made with volcanic rock, a molcajete is similar to a mortar and pestle and is perfect for grinding herbs and chiles. If you don't wish to invest in a molcajete, a blender or spice grinder will do the trick.

Tortilla press: The tortilla press helps you create consistently sized tortillas easily and quickly. You can certainly make tortillas without one, but they'll be less uniform.

Propane torch: This handy kitchen tool is indispensable once you get used to it. You can brown meringues, caramelize sugar on the tops of desserts, fire-roast onions and peppers, and perform many other kitchen tasks. The torches sold for kitchen use tend to be small, so look for a torch with at least a 14-ounce propane cylinder.

THIS BOOK'S RECIPES

It should be easy enough to follow and successfully make any of the recipes in this book, but here's a little guide to what you can expect to see with the recipes—and why.

Prep Time
This covers the amount of time you'll spend chopping, slicing, and dicing meat, vegetables, or fruit before tossing it in the slow cooker. I've made an effort to limit prep time to no more than 20 minutes throughout the book.

Cook Time
This refers to the cooking that takes place in the slow cooker. Some recipes will include two cook times—one for slow cooking on high and one for slow cooking on low—when possible. Many people like to cook on low so that they can begin a slow cooker meal in the morning and come back to it at the end of the day, so that's why two options will be given if they make sense. If it's recommended that you cook only on low or high, only one time (and heat level) will be indicated.

Any recipe that offers a cook time of 6 hours or more on *low* (even if it also offers an option for a shorter cooking time on high) will have the pre-slow-cooking prep instructions broken out from the slow cooking instructions. Why? Because I recommend prepping the ingredients for long-cooking recipes the night before so that you can throw them in the slow cooker in the morning and go out for a long stretch of time. These recipes will have cooking instructions separated by these headings:

The Night Before
In the Morning

Recipes that cook for shorter times (whether on low or high) are easy to prep and cook the same day, and their instructions aren't broken out.

It would be great if all slow cooker recipes took 8 hours or more to cook, allowing us to go about our days as we please. But the reality is that some fantastic slow-cooker foods—such as dips, fish dishes, some vegetables, and desserts—simply don't need that much time in the cooker. They'll overcook. So keep in mind that there will be some recipes in this book that will cook only for 2, 4, or 6 hours. These are ones you might prefer to make on the weekend. They don't need constant monitoring, but you can't leave the house for the entire day.

Heat Level

Some like it hot—and some really don't. Unless a recipe is completely free of heat, you'll see one to four chiles to indicate just how hot you can expect the finished dish to be. Here's what each chile indicates:

    ♦ Mild

    ♦♦ Medium

    ♦♦♦ Hot

    ♦♦♦♦ **En Fuego** (translation: *on fire*)

Tips

Keep an eye out for recipe tips that'll offer pre-cooking instructions if you have time for them, ingredient substitutions, warnings, and other useful tidbits designed to help you make these recipes easily and successfully.

CHILE TRIVIA

Mexican cooking is all about community and joy through food. Here are some fun facts about chiles that are sure to get the conversation started at mealtimes or fiestas.

- Chiles have more vitamin C than oranges.

- The most effective way to cool your mouth after a bite of a hot chile is to eat sour cream or ice cream.

- For more than 20 years, salsa has outsold ketchup in the United States.

- Capsaicin is the stuff that makes chiles hot. Pure capsaicin is insoluble in cold water, so drink warm water or another beverage to stop your mouth from burning.

- Chiles, much like cacao beans, were once so valued by the Aztec and Maya that they were used as currency.

- George Washington and Thomas Jefferson both grew chiles.

- If a chile is cut open and has reddish-orange areas, it's an especially potent one, hotter than a typical chile of the same variety.

3

DIPS AND APPETIZERS

Dips and sauces are best cooked in a small 1½- or 2-quart slow cooker. If you plan on making mostly dips and sauces in this secondary appliance, buy a round one: it will heat liquids more evenly than an oval one can. If your gatherings generally include fewer than 10 people, the smallest size is fine. If you have larger parties, then a 2-quart or larger slow cooker is probably better.

CHEESE DIP WITH MEAT

Queso con Carne

SERVES 16 · PREP TIME: 20 MINUTES · COOK TIME: 2 HOURS (LOW)

♥♥♥ This queso with meat is spicy and hearty. Highly seasoned lean ground beef is added to the creamy cheese mixture along with smoky chipotle and roasted jalapeños. You'll definitely notice a flavor difference when you compare it to the dips made with processed cheese. Note that, to save time, this recipe does not call for pre-cooking ingredients before adding them to the slow cooker. That said, browning the beef and sautéing the onion will deepen the flavor of the dip. See the Tip for optional pre-cooking instructions.

1 pound lean ground beef

1 medium onion, chopped

1 large tomato, seeded and chopped

3 medium roasted jalapeños, peeled, seeded, and chopped (see page 158)

1 tablespoon Taco Seasoning Mix (see page 156)

1 to 2 chipotles in adobo, chopped to a paste, to taste

Cooking spray

1 cup whole milk

8 ounces queso quesadilla or cream cheese, cut into 1-inch cubes

1 cup grated Monterey Jack cheese

½ cup grated Cheddar cheese

1. In a large bowl, add the ground beef, onion, tomato, and jalapeños. Stir the ingredients. Add in the seasoning mix and then the chopped chipotles, and then stir again.

2. Spray the inside of the slow cooker with cooking spray. Add the meat-vegetable mixture to the cooker and then stir in the milk and cheeses with a wooden spoon.

3. Cover and cook on low for 2 hours. Stir the cheese dip again and serve.

Pre-Cooking Tip: In a large frying pan over medium-high heat, heat ¼ cup of olive oil. Add the ground beef and cook it until it is thoroughly browned, then transfer the beef to a large bowl. Pour all but about 1 tablespoon of olive oil out of the frying pan, and then return the pan to the heat. Add the onion to it, and sauté quickly for 2 minutes, or until it is softened. Add the cooked onion to the bowl with beef, and stir in the tomato, jalapeños, seasoning mix, and chipotles. Once mixed, follow the instructions in step 2.

TWO-CHILE CHEESE DIP

Queso Dos Chiles

SERVES 16 ● PREP TIME: 20 MINUTES ● COOK TIME: 2 HOURS (LOW)

❦ *This is a classic Tex-Mex dip. This smooth and creamy version adds jalapeño and poblano chiles to give it a kick. Queso is traditionally served with tortilla chips, but there are endless possibilities—consider boiled or roasted fingerling potatoes for a unique, nontraditional dipper. Queso quesadilla is a mild, white melting cheese. If you can't find it at your grocery store, you can substitute full-fat cream cheese.*

Cooking spray

1 medium onion, chopped

1 large tomato, seeded and chopped

3 medium jalapeños, seeded and chopped

1 medium poblano chile, seeded and chopped

1 garlic clove, minced

1 cup whole milk

8 ounces queso quesadilla or cream cheese, cut into 1-inch cubes

8 ounces grated American cheese, white or yellow

1. Spray the inside of the slow cooker with cooking spray, then add the onion, tomato, jalapeños, poblano chile, garlic, milk, and cheeses to the slow cooker. Give everything a quick stir with a wooden spoon.

2. Cover and cook on low for 2 hours. When the cooking finishes, stir the dip and serve.

Pre-Cooking Tip: In a medium-size frying pan over medium-high heat, melt 2 tablespoons of unsalted butter. Add the onion, tomato, jalapeños, poblano chile, and garlic to the pan and sauté until the vegetables soften a little. Continue with step 1 of the recipe.

Ingredient Variation: Vine-ripened tomatoes and fresh jalapeños give this dish authenticity and intense flavor, but if they are out of season or if you need to save time, you can easily substitute canned diced tomatoes and canned chiles. Just be sure to drain them well.

CHICKEN NACHO DIP

Dip Estilo Nachos de Pollo

SERVES 16 ◦ PREP TIME: 5 MINUTES ◦ COOK TIME: 4 HOURS (LOW)

♥♥♥ *This hot-and-spicy dip is especially quick to put together. The sour cream adds a little tang, but you can substitute plain Greek yogurt. Fresh jalapeños are added without pre-cooking so they maintain their shape and a little of their crispness. Pepper Jack cheese adds creaminess, flavor, and heat, but if you like it really spicy, substitute habanero Jack cheese for the pepper Jack. Serve with some diced avocado on the side.*

1 large tomato, diced

3 medium jalapeños, seeded and chopped

1½ cups shredded cooked chicken

1 tablespoon cornstarch

4 ounces grated pepper Jack cheese

4 ounces grated Cheddar cheese

1 (12-ounce) can evaporated milk

⅓ cup sour cream

¼ cup diced scallions

1 tablespoon Taco Seasoning Mix (see page 156)

½ cup fresh or frozen corn

1 cup cooked black beans, drained and rinsed

1. In the slow cooker, combine all the ingredients, stirring with a wooden spoon to blend.

2. Cook on low for 4 hours.

3. Give the dip another quick stir. If the dip is not thick enough, remove the lid and cook for 30 minutes more.

4. Stir it again and serve hot.

CORN AND CHEESE DIP

Dip de Elote con Queso

SERVES 16 • PREP TIME: 5 MINUTES • COOK TIME: 4 HOURS (LOW)

In this dip, sweet corn is enrobed in a rich, silky cheese sauce with bursts of heat from jalapeños and poblano chiles. Chopped cilantro and lime juice tossed in at the end of cooking add fresh flavor. This dip goes with everything, and it's likely that if the chips run out, your guests will finish it off with spoons. For a delicious, smoky variation, stir in about ½ pound of crispy cooked bacon just before serving.

4½ cups fresh or frozen corn

2 jalapeños, seeded and diced

½ small poblano chile, seeded and diced (about ¼ cup)

½ cup sour cream

1 cup grated pepper Jack cheese

8 ounces cream cheese, cut into 1-inch cubes

1 tablespoon Taco Seasoning Mix (see page 156)

½ teaspoon ground cumin

1 cup chopped fresh cilantro

Juice of 1 lime

1. In the slow cooker, combine everything but the cilantro and lime juice.

2. Cover and cook on low for 4 hours.

3. Remove the lid, stir with a wooden spoon, and add the cilantro. Squeeze the lime juice over the top and serve hot.

FIRE-ROASTED ENCHILADA SAUCE

Salsa Asada Sencilla para Enchiladas

This recipe for spicy enchilada sauce makes a lot, but you can freeze it in recipe-size portions. Chipotles have their own pleasant smokiness, which combines with the fire-roasted tomatoes to create a sauce that tastes like it has been simmering over a mesquite fire all day long. Onions, bell peppers, garlic, and cumin add the perfect balance of depth and richness. For a less spicy sauce, remove and discard the chipotles before blending the sauce. You can fire roast your own tomatoes, but the canned ones are delicious and save quite a bit of time.

1 (7-ounce) can chipotles in adobo, seeded

2 cups Chicken Stock (see page 46)

1 (32-ounce) can fire-roasted tomatoes

4 medium onions, chopped

1 medium bell pepper (any color), seeded and diced (about 1 cup)

5 garlic cloves, minced

1 tablespoon ground cumin

1½ teaspoons chili powder

1 teaspoon sugar

1. Measure out 3 tablespoons of adobo sauce and set it aside. Put the remaining adobo sauce in a nonreactive bowl and store it in the refrigerator for future use.

2. In the slow cooker, combine all the remaining ingredients, and cook on low for 8 hours or on high for 4 hours.

3. Blend the sauce in a blender until smooth, 2 cups at a time. Plan to use about 1 to 1½ cups of sauce for every 8 to 10 enchiladas you make.

4. Freeze unused sauce in 1-cup portions, leaving some room in your resealable freezer bags for some expansion. Then put the portion in the refrigerator to thaw the night before you plan to use it on the next batch of enchiladas.

Warning: Blend the hot sauce in your blender in small batches. If you put too much in the blender, pressure will build up because of the steam, and the top might fly off unexpectedly, burning you and anyone else nearby.

RED SALSA

Salsa Roja

MAKES 3 CUPS ○ PREP TIME: 5 MINUTES ○ COOK TIME: 6 HOURS (LOW), 3 HOURS (HIGH)

Fresh raw salsas are delicious, but they can't be made ahead and frozen for later use without losing their bright flavors and crisp textures. This red salsa is cooked, so it freezes well. The recipe can be doubled or tripled, and you can freeze it for up to 3 months without any change in flavor or texture.

2 pounds Roma tomatoes

1 onion, cut into quarters

3 jalapeños, stems removed

2 garlic cloves

1 bunch fresh cilantro, stems removed

Juice of 1 lime

Sea salt

1. In the slow cooker, combine the tomatoes, onion, jalapeños, and garlic, and cook on low for 6 hours or on high for 3 hours.

2. Pour 2 cups of the salsa into a food processor or blender, add one-third of the cilantro, and pulse the mixture a few times to combine. Pour the salsa into a large bowl and repeat until all the tomato mixture and all the cilantro has been used.

3. Squeeze the lime juice over the salsa, and stir gently with a wooden spoon to blend. Season with salt to taste.

4. Keep the salsa refrigerated in a tightly sealed, nonreactive container for up to 1 week, or freeze it for up to 3 months.

JALAPEÑO POPPERS

Jalapeños Rellenos

MAKES 24 POPPERS · PREP TIME: 15 MINUTES ·
COOK TIME: 4 HOURS (LOW), 2 HOURS (HIGH)

Jalapeño poppers are not an authentic Mexican food, but they do have authentic Mexican flavors, and they are a cinch to make. A mixture of cream cheese and Cheddar cheese is spooned into jalapeño halves, which are then wrapped in bacon. While they cook, the juices from the spicy jalapeños and the smoky bacon infuse the cheese with flavor. Because this is a moist-heat type of cooking, the bacon won't get crispy. If you want, you can remove the bacon after cooking or leave it off altogether. Another option is to cook the bacon until it is crisp and then mix it in with the cheese.

8 ounces cream cheese, at room
  temperature

¼ cup sour cream

¼ cup grated Cheddar cheese

12 jalapeños, washed, seeded,
  and halved lengthwise

24 slices bacon

⅓ cup Chicken Stock (see page 46)
  or water

1. In a medium bowl, mix together the cream cheese, sour cream, and grated Cheddar cheese until well blended.

2. Divide the cheese mixture evenly among the jalapeño halves, and wrap each stuffed jalapeño half with a slice of bacon; secure the bacon with a toothpick.

3. In the slow cooker, pour in the chicken stock and add the stuffed jalapeños.

4. Cover and cook on low for 4 hours or on high for 2 hours.

5. Using a slotted spoon, remove the stuffed jalapeños from the slow cooker and serve hot or at room temperature.

Warning: Always wear gloves when you are working with jalapeños. The same oils in the peppers that make them burn your tongue will burn your fingers. Also, never touch your eyes or any other sensitive area without first removing your gloves and washing your hands.

SPICY CHICKEN NACHOS

Nachos de Pollo Picantes

SERVES 8 • PREP TIME: 15 MINUTES • COOK TIME: 8 HOURS (LOW), 4 HOURS (HIGH)

These nachos work well as an appetizer, a snack, or a quick dinner. There's plenty of protein from the chicken, black beans, and cheese. If you have the time, dice the chicken breast before putting it in the cooker. It will add a few extra minutes of preparation, but the end result will be prettier than the shredded chicken. Make the nachos spicier by adding a tablespoon or two of chipotles in adobo. Traditionally, nacho toppings are served on tortilla chips, but you can spoon this on baked potatoes, tortillas, omelets, or almost anything else you can think of. Use your imagination.

2 pounds boneless, skinless chicken breast

2 large tomatoes, diced

1 medium onion, chopped

3 medium jalapeños, seeded and chopped

1 cup cooked black beans, drained and rinsed

1 tablespoon chili power

½ teaspoon garlic powder

½ teaspoon sea salt

½ teaspoon freshly ground black pepper

1 tablespoon packed brown sugar

½ cup Chicken Stock (see page 46)

8 ounces grated pepper Jack cheese

8 ounces grated Colby or Cheddar cheese

Tortilla chips

Sliced jalapeños, olives, and other favorite nacho toppings

1. In the slow cooker, combine the chicken, tomatoes, onion, and jalapeños. Spoon the black beans over the chicken and vegetables.

2. In a medium bowl, mix together the chili powder, garlic powder, salt, black pepper, brown sugar, and chicken stock. Pour the mixture over the chicken, vegetables, and beans.

3. Sprinkle the cheeses over the top.

4. Cover and cook on low for 8 hours or on high for 4 hours.

5. Remove the lid and shred the chicken, then mix it back in with the other ingredients. Serve hot with tortilla chips and your favorite toppings.

Diet Variation: If you are vegetarian, swap out the chicken for double the amount of beans or add 2 cups of chopped tempeh, and replace the Chicken Stock with Vegetable Stock (page 48). To give the dish deeper flavor than you can get with the beans alone, add in 1 cup of corn, too.

4

STOCKS AND SOUPS

~~~~~~~~~~~~~~~~~~

Stocks and soups have been staples of Mexican cooking since well before the Spaniards set foot on Mexican shores. Cooking pots filled with meat bones, aromatics, and water were hung over fires to simmer all day. Vegetables were added as they came in season, and from this basic cooking method came the hearty sopas and pozoles, rich with hominy, vegetables, herbs, and ground corn and nuts.

Basic stocks are essential for sauces as well as soups and stews. Stocks are different from broths in that they are made with meat, while stocks are made with bones, aromatics, and vegetables for flavor. Having a slow cooker makes it much easier to create flavorful stocks and soups even when you are not at home. You don't even have to peel the vegetables; just wash and quarter them if they are large. Toss everything in your slow cooker for 8 to 10 hours and then strain the flavorful broth so you can use it as you like.

CHICKEN STOCK

Consomé de Pollo

MAKES 3 QUARTS • PREP TIME: 15 MINUTES •
COOK TIME: 10 HOURS (LOW), 5 HOURS (HIGH)

Once you make your own stock with your slow cooker, you won't want to buy it from the store ever again. Homemade chicken stock is rich with the flavors of chicken, herbs, spices, and vegetables, so it really enhances the flavors of the dishes you use it in. The serrano chile brings heat to the stock, and the chipotle gives it that classic smokiness. Press the juices out of the vegetables and meat when you strain the stock so you get every bit of flavor. Keep the cooked chicken for other dishes, but toss the vegetables out in the compost pile.

3 pounds bone-in, skinless chicken thighs, fat removed

1 onions, peeled and quartered

2 garlic cloves, halved

1 serrano chile, halved and seeded

1 dried chipotle, halved and seeded

2 carrots

2 bay leaves

12 stems fresh cilantro

2 stems fresh thyme

1 gallons water

1 teapoon sea salt

1. In the slow cooker, combine all the ingredients.

2. Cover and cook on low for 10 hours or on high for 5 hours. Turn off the slow cooker and let the stock cool for about 1 hour.

3. Place a large colander over a large bowl. Pour the stock through the colander to strain it.

4. Taste the stock and add more salt if necessary.

5. Ladle the stock into storage containers and cover them tightly. Store the stock in the refrigerator for up to 1 week or in the freezer indefinitely.

6. Skim off any fat before using.

BEEF STOCK

Consomé de Res

MAKES 4 QUARTS • PREP TIME: 15 MINUTES •
COOK TIME: 10 HOURS (LOW), 5 HOURS (HIGH)

Beef stock is an important ingredient in numerous recipes. Like Chicken Stock, it's easy to make, and it freezes well so you can always have it on hand. Using beef bones as well as meat gives the stock a depth and richness, while the chiles add smokiness and heat. If you leave the seeds in the chiles, the stock will be much spicier than if you take them out. Either way is perfectly acceptable. When the stock is done, save the meat for use in soups or season it to use in tacos or enchiladas.

1 onion, peeled and quartered

4 garlic cloves, halved

2 Roma tomatoes

1 dried chipotle

1 dried mulato chile

1 carrot

1 bay leaf

½ teaspoon peppercorns

10 stems fresh cilantro

½ teaspoon ground cumin

3 pounds beef shin bones, cut in 2-inch lengths (your butcher can do this)

1 pound lean beef chuck roast

1 gallon water

2 teaspoons sea salt

1. In the slow cooker, combine all ingredients.

2. Cover and cook on low for 10 hours or on high for 5 hours. Turn off the slow cooker and let the stock cool for about 1 hour.

3. Place a colander over a large bowl and strain the stock through the colander.

4. Taste the stock and add more salt and/or pepper if necessary.

5. Ladle the stock into storage containers and cover them tightly. Store the stock in the refrigerator for up to 1 week or in the freezer indefinitely.

6. Skim off any fat before using.

   Pre-Cooking Tip: Roasting the shin bones before using them in the stock will give you significantly more flavor. To roast them, preheat your oven to 400°F. Place the bones in a roasting pan and roast them for 1½ hours, turning them every 10 or 15 minutes. Don't let them burn.

VEGETABLE STOCK

Consomé de Verduras

MAKES 2½ QUARTS • PREP TIME: 5 MINUTES •
COOK TIME: 10 HOURS (LOW), 5 HOURS (HIGH)

Vegetable stock can be used interchangeably with beef or chicken stock in most recipes. It's a good way to make many Mexican dishes vegetarian. This intensely flavored stock is a complex marriage of the fresh flavors of Mexico, with a delicate balance of garlic, cilantro, and cumin. The chipotle gives it a little heat, while the mushrooms add a pleasant meaty flavor to the blend. If you happen to have corn cobs (with or without corn kernels), add one or two of them for sweetness. Pressing the vegetables as you strain the stock will yield more flavor, but your stock will be cloudier than it would be without pressing.

2 onions, peeled and quartered

3 garlic cloves, halved

6 celery stalks

4 carrots

½ pound cremini or button mushrooms

3 Roma tomatoes

10 cilantro stems

1 dried chipotle

1 teaspoon ground cumin

1 tablespoon peppercorns

2 bay leaves

3 quarts water

1. In the slow cooker, combine all the ingredients.

2. Cover and cook on low for 10 hours or on high for 5 hours. Turn off the slow cooker and let the stock cool for about 1 hour.

3. Place a colander over a large bowl and strain the stock through the colander, pressing the vegetables to get as much flavor as possible. Discard the vegetables.

4. Ladle the stock into storage containers and cover them tightly. Store the stock in the refrigerator for up to 1 week or in the freezer indefinitely.

Pre-Cooking Tip: If you have the time and would like even more flavor in this stock, toss the vegetables with a tablespoon or so of olive oil and roast them at 400°F for 10 to 15 minutes, or until they have browned a little. Use them as directed in the recipe.

CHICKEN SOUP

Caldo de Pollo

SERVES 6 * PREP TIME: 20 MINUTES * COOK TIME: 8 HOURS (LOW)

Most cultures have some form of chicken soup, and with good reason. It's inexpensive, it's comforting, and most of all it is delicious. This version has plenty of vegetables for a hearty and healing bowl. Traditionally, corn is left on the cob, but you can use a cup of corn kernels for easier eating. To bump up the heat, go ahead and add 1 or 2 chopped and seeded jalapeños into the slow cooker with the rest of the vegetables. If you have cooked rice on hand, you may want to add it to the bottom of your bowl before ladling in the soup to make a more filling meal.

8 cups Chicken Stock (page 46)

1 medium cabbage, cut into wedges

1½ pounds boneless chicken breast or thighs

4 potatoes, peeled and cubed

4 carrots, peeled and sliced

1 small onion, chopped

2 jalapeños, chopped and seeded

1 zucchini, diced

2 ears fresh corn, cut in 3 pieces each

1 (14.5-ounce) can stewed tomatoes, undrained

⅓ cup fresh cilantro, chopped

1. In the slow cooker, add all of the ingredients except the cilantro.

2. Cover and cook on low for 8 hours.

3. Remove the lid and take out the chicken. Shred it and then add it back to the cooker before serving. Then ladle the soup into bowls and garnish with the cilantro to serve.

CHICKEN AND TORTILLA SOUP

Sopa de Pollo con Tortilla

SERVES 6 • PREP TIME: 15 MINUTES • COOK TIME: 8 HOURS (LOW), 4 HOURS (HIGH)

Chicken and Tortilla Soup is a hearty dish that's made with shredded chicken, black beans, and corn in a spicy chicken stock flavored with plenty of garlic and cilantro. You can adjust the heat of this dish by adding more ancho chiles or jalapeños to taste. The tortilla chips not only add crunch, but they also thicken the soup and add flavor. The melting cheese and cool sour cream add texture and balance to the spicy heat of the chiles. If you'd like it a little spicier, substitute pepper Jack cheese for the Cheddar. Once you taste your first spoonful of this soup, you will understand why it's such a favorite on so many restaurant menus.

1½ pounds boneless, skinless chicken breasts or thighs

2 onions, chopped

4 garlic cloves, minced

1 medium bell pepper (any color), chopped

2 teaspoons chili powder

1 teaspoon dried oregano

1 dried ancho chile

4 large tomatoes, diced

3 medium jalapeños, seeded and chopped

4 cups Chicken Stock (see page 46)

2 cups fresh or frozen corn

3 cups cooked black beans

½ cup chopped fresh cilantro

1 cup coarsely chopped tortilla chips

2 cups grated Cheddar cheese

½ cup sour cream

1. In the slow cooker, combine all the ingredients except the chips, cheese, and sour cream.

2. Cover and cook on low for 8 hours or on high for 4 hours.

3. Remove the ancho chile from the soup. Transfer the chicken to a cutting board and shred it using two forks; stir the shredded chicken back into the soup.

4. Ladle the soup into bowls and top with the chips, cheese, and sour cream.

Time-saving Tip: Replace the fresh tomatoes and jalapeños with 3 (14.5-ounce) cans of diced tomatoes with chiles. You can also use canned black, pinto, or kidney beans if you prefer.

CHICKEN FAJITA CHILI

Chili de Pollo Estilo Fajita

SERVES 6 • PREP TIME: 10 MINUTES • COOK TIME: 8 HOURS (LOW), 4 HOURS (HIGH)

♥♥♥ *This chili blends two favorites into one soul-warming dish, making it perfect for blustery winter days. Serve this spicy chili with warm whole-grain tortillas and a crispy romaine salad. The chipotles in adobo are what makes this chili hot—if you'd prefer it milder, cut back on the chipotle or leave it out altogether. Chicken thighs are less expensive and stand up better to the bold flavors of this dish, but you can certainly use chicken breasts instead if you prefer white meat. If tomatoes are out of season, buy canned diced fire-roasted tomatoes. The roasted flavor really works in the dish.*

2 pounds boneless, skinless chicken thighs, cut into bite-size pieces

1 tablespoon chili powder

2 teaspoons Fajita Seasoning Mix (see page 157)

2 garlic cloves, minced

1 teaspoon ground cumin

2 large tomatoes, diced

1 large poblano chile, seeded and diced

1 tablespoon chopped chipotles in adobo

2 cups cooked red kidney beans

1½ cups Chicken Stock (see page 46)

⅓ cup grated Cheddar cheese

1. In the slow cooker, combine all the ingredients except the cheese.

2. Cover and cook on low for 8 hours or on high for 4 hours.

3. Stir the soup with a wooden spoon to blend, and then ladle the soup into bowls. Top the soup with the cheese before serving.

SPICY CHICKEN AND CHICKPEA SOUP

Caldo Tlalpeño

SERVES 6 • PREP TIME: 10 MINUTES • COOK TIME: 7 HOURS ON LOW

❦❦❦ *This soup is a traditional Mexican dish that offers a mix of vegetables in a smoky and spicy broth. Because chipotle tends to intensify in flavor the longer it cooks, the recipe calls for putting it in the slow cooker during the last hour of cooking. If you and your family love heat, you can certainly put it in with the rest of the ingredients when you begin. If spice isn't your thing, leave out the chipotle and add just a teaspoon of mashed chipotle and adobo to the bowl when serving.*

2 quarts Chicken Stock (see page 46)

1½ pounds boneless chicken breast or thighs

2 small onions, chopped

2 large garlic cloves, chopped

1 sprig fresh epazote or 1 teaspoon dried

1 large carrot, diced

½ cup long-grain brown rice (uncooked)

2 tablespoons olive oil

2 (14.5-ounce) cans diced tomatoes

½ cup cooked chickpeas

½ teaspoon Mexican oregano

2 bay leaves

2 chipotles in adobo

1 tablespoon adobo sauce

Pinch salt

2 avocados, chopped

⅓ cup fresh cilantro, chopped

⅓ cup crumbled queso fresco

2 limes, cut into wedges

1. In the slow cooker, add all of the ingredients up through the bay leaves.

2. Cover and cook on low for 6 hours.

3. Lift the lid and remove the chicken. Using a fork, shred it and place it back in the slow cooker. Add the chipotles and adobo and cook for 1 hour more.

4. Taste the soup and add salt as needed. Remove the bay leaves.

5. Serve in individual bowls topped with the avocado, cilantro, and queso fresco. Juice from the lime wedges may be added as desired.

Ingredient Tip: The epazote herb is well known in Mexico for the tangy flavor it adds to soups, moles, and dishes containing beans. Dried epazote is available at many grocers and online (check out penzeys.com). Use 1 teaspoon of dried epazote in place of 1 fresh sprig in any recipe. If you find you don't care for it, feel free to leave it out.

BEEF POZOLE

Pozole de Res

SERVES 6 • PREP TIME: 15 MINUTES • COOK TIME: 8 HOURS (LOW), 4 HOURS (HIGH)

❦ *Pozole is a traditional Mexican soup, almost a stew, that is often served on Sundays or special occasions like Independence Day (September 16). It is spicy and meaty, with a generous amount of hominy, which is corn that has been soaked in limewater. Pozole is traditionally served with tortillas and garnished with crunchy cabbage, spicy radishes, creamy avocados, and acidic limes to give it a pop of freshness. This dish calls for Mexican oregano, as do a handful of other recipes in this book. It has a slight citrus flavor but is similar enough to Mediterranean oregano that you can use them interchangeably.*

1 dried pasilla chile

3 cups Beef Stock (see page 47)

1½ pounds lean, boneless beef roast, cut into bite-size pieces

2 medium onions, chopped

4 garlic cloves, minced

3 medium jalapeños, seeded and sliced

2 (15-ounce) cans white or yellow hominy, drained

2 teaspoons ground cumin

1 teaspoon dried Mexican oregano

TOPPINGS

½ head green or red cabbage, shredded

1 bunch fresh cilantro, chopped

2 avocados, diced

2 limes, cut into wedges

1 bunch radishes, trimmed and thinly sliced

The Night Before

1. In a heavy cast iron or stainless steel frying pan heated to hot over medium-high heat, add the pasilla chile and roast it on all sides until it is pliable and fragrant, 1 to 2 minutes total. Add ½ cup of beef stock to the pan and allow it to come to a boil. Turn off the heat and let the mixture stand for 5 minutes.

2. Transfer the chile and stock to a blender and process until smooth. Refrigerate the blended chile mixture in a tightly sealed container.

In the Morning

1. In the slow cooker, add the chili mixture and all the other ingredients except the toppings.

2. Cover and cook on low for 8 hours or on high for 4 hours.

3. Stir the pozole with a wooden spoon to blend, and then ladle it into bowls. Serve immediately, passing the toppings at the table.

MEATBALL SOUP

Sopa de Albóndigas

SERVES 6 * PREP TIME: 20 MINUTES * COOK TIME: 8 HOURS (LOW), 4 HOURS (HIGH)

This classic soup features seasoned meatballs cooked in a spicy beef stock until they are tender and have soaked up the flavors in the liquid. You can use commercially prepared beef broth and frozen meatballs to save time, but you'll miss out on flavor. If you use the Beef Stock recipe (page 47), which is a bit spicy on its own, you might want to cut back on the guajillo and ancho chiles used here, depending on how much fire you like in your mouth. If you are using commercial broth, you'll definitely need all of the chiles for flavor.

FOR THE MEATBALLS

1½ pounds lean ground beef

1½ tablespoons minced fresh cilantro

1½ tablespoons minced onion

1½ tablespoons minced poblano chile

¼ cup unseasoned breadcrumbs

1 teaspoon sea salt

3 eggs

FOR THE SOUP

3 dried ancho chiles

3 dried guajillo chiles

8 cups Beef Stock (see page 47)

2 Roma tomatoes, diced

4 garlic cloves, chopped

1 medium onion, chopped

2 medium carrots, sliced

1 teaspoon ground cumin

Sea salt, to taste

The Night Before

1. In a large bowl, mix together all the meatball ingredients. Gently form 24 meatballs, using about 1 tablespoon of the mixture for each meatball.

2. Place the meatballs on a baking sheet in a single layer; cover and refrigerate overnight.

In the Morning

1. In the slow cooker, combine all the soup ingredients and the meatballs.

2. Cover and and cook on low for 8 hours or on high for 4 hours. Remove and discard the chiles from the pot. Taste and adjust the seasonings as needed.

3. Serve the soup hot in large bowls.

SMOKY BEAN AND BEEF SOUP

Sopa de Res con Frijoles

SERVES 8 ○ PREP TIME: 15 MINUTES ○ COOK TIME: 8 HOURS (LOW), 4 HOURS (HIGH)

Although using all fresh ingredients is a good rule of thumb, there are times when you need the ease of opening a few cans. This soup is delicious, and if you keep recipe-size portions of cooked ground beef in the freezer, it goes together even faster. Ranch-style beans are known for their smoky flavor. They add richness to this soup, but if you can't find them, pinto or kidney beans will work just fine. Top each bowl with a dollop of sour cream, some salsa, and diced avocado to add cool yet rich flavors.

1½ pounds lean ground beef

1 medium onion, chopped

2 (15-ounce) cans ranch-style beans

2 (14.5-ounce) cans diced tomatoes
    with chiles

2 cups fresh or frozen corn

2 tablespoons Taco Seasoning Mix
    (see page 156)

1 cup Beef Stock (see page 47)

TOPPINGS

½ cup grated Cheddar cheese

Sour cream

Salsa

Diced avocado

1. In the slow cooker, combine all of the ingredients except the toppings.

2. Cover and cook on low for 8 hours or on high for 4 hours.

3. Stir the soup with a wooden spoon to blend and ladle it into bowls. Sprinkle with the grated cheese before serving, and pass the sour cream, salsa, and avocado at the table.

Pre-Cooking Tip: Place a medium skillet over medium-high heat and cook the ground beef until it is thoroughly browned, 3 to 4 minutes. Then follow the instructions in step 1.

GREEN CHILE AND PORK POZOLE

Pozole Verde de Puerco

SERVES 8 · PREP TIME: 5 MINUTES · COOK TIME: 10 HOURS (LOW), 5 HOURS (HIGH)

❦❦❦ Pozole verde, *or green pozole, is Mexican comfort food and, in this version, is quite spicy. The broth is flavorful, with a lot of heat and a fresh flavor that comes from the limes and cilantro. This is a light dish that will warm you to your core on a cold day but won't make you feel overly full. Leftovers freeze well for up to 6 months.*

2½ pounds lean, boneless pork, cut into bite-size pieces

2 teaspoons ground cumin

1 cup Chicken Stock (see page 46)

3 medium onions, chopped

3 jalapeños, seeded and chopped

1 (28-ounce) can white hominy, drained

2 (28-ounce) cans tomatillos, drained

1 bunch fresh cilantro, chopped, plus more for garnish

1 teaspoon sugar (optional)

2 limes, cut into wedges

1. In the slow cooker, combine all the ingredients except the limes.

2. Cover and cook on low for 10 hours or on high for 5 hours.

3. Taste the broth and add sugar if needed to balance the acidity of the tomatillos.

4. Serve in bowls garnished with more cilantro and limes wedges for squeezing into the soup.

Ingredient Tip: Tomatillos are small, round fruits that resemble green tomatoes wrapped in a papery husk. They have a tart, tangy flavor and are used for green salsa. Many grocery stores in the Southwest carry them fresh or canned, but if you can't find them, commercially prepared green salsa is a good substitute.

CREAMY CORN CHOWDER

Crema de Elote

SERVES 8 • PREP TIME: 15 MINUTES • COOK TIME: 8 HOURS (LOW), 4 HOURS (HIGH)

Corn was one of the staple foods of the indigenous peoples of Mexico. This warming soup captures the flavors of that rich heritage. It's smooth, creamy, and full of sweet corn flavor with just enough spicy heat to make it interesting. The warm flavor of cumin enhances every bite. Add cooked chicken breast or bacon to make this a heartier soup if you wish. The bacon is best cooked crispy, crumbled, and sprinkled on the top just before serving. A side salad with vinaigrette dressing complements the flavors of this soup.

4 poblano chiles, fire-roasted (see page 158), peeled, and seeded

2 medium onions, chopped

3 garlic cloves, minced

½ teaspoon ground cumin

2 cups Chicken Stock (see page 46)

2 (14.5-ounce) cans cream-style corn

2 cups fresh or frozen corn

1 medium russet potato, peeled and diced

1 cup heavy cream or half-and-half

½ cup chopped fresh cilantro

1. In the slow cooker, combine the roasted chiles and the remaining ingredients, except the cream and cilantro.

2. Cover and cook on low for 8 hours or on high for 4 hours.

3. Stir in the cream. Taste and adjust the seasonings as necessary. Serve topped with the chopped cilantro.

BLACK BEAN SOUP WITH CHIPOTLE

Sopa de Frijol con Chipotle

SERVES 8 ◦ PREP TIME: 10 MINUTES, PLUS SOAKING TIME ◦ COOK TIME: 10 HOURS (LOW)

♦♦♦ *There's no need to start with cooked beans in this easy recipe. Black beans are cooked right in the slow cooker with tomatoes, garlic, spices, and a generous amount of smoky chipotle for just the right kick. You'll need an immersion or traditional blender to make the soup smooth before serving. It should look almost like chocolate pudding.*

1 pound dried black beans

6 Roma tomatoes, diced

2 garlic cloves, chopped

3 tablespoons chopped chipotles in adobo

1 teaspoon ground cinnamon

1 tablespoon ground cumin

Juice of 1 orange

Juice of 1 lime

½ cup chopped fresh cilantro

5 cups Vegetable Stock (see page 48)

2 limes, cut into wedges

The Night Before

Place the beans in a large bowl and cover them with water. Let them soak overnight at room temperature.

In the Morning

1. Drain and rinse the beans.

2. In the slow cooker, combine all the ingredients except the cilantro and lime wedges.

3. Cover and cook on low for 10 hours.

4. When the beans are very soft, blend the soup with a handheld immersion blender until smooth, or blend it in batches in a blender. Stir in the chopped cilantro.

5. Ladle the soup into bowls and serve hot with the lime wedges.

Time-saving Tip: If you choose to use cooked beans in this recipe, use 6 cups and reduce the stock to 3 cups. Cook the soup on low for 4 hours or on high for 2 hours. Follow the instructions in the recipe for blending and serving.

CHAYOTE AND POBLANO SOUP

Sopa de Chayote y Chile Poblano

SERVES 6 • PREP TIME: 20 MINUTES • COOK TIME: 6 HOURS (LOW), 3 HOURS (HIGH)

This is a light, fresh-tasting vegetable soup that works well as a first course. Chicken can be added to this basic recipe to make it more filling and to bump up the protein. If you'd like to give it more body, transfer about 1½ cups of the finished soup to a blender, leaving the black beans in the pot, and blend it until smooth. Pour this mixture back into the slow cooker and stir gently before serving. This dish goes especially well with grilled shrimp and seafood, a loaf of crusty bread, and some grilled fruit. This is one of those recipes that are better the next day.

1 medium onion, chopped

4 garlic cloves, minced

4 cups Chicken Stock (see page 47) or Vegetable Stock (see page 48)

1 small poblano chile (or ½ medium), seeded and chopped

2 chayotes, pitted, peeled, and diced

¼ cup diced red bell pepper

½ cup diced green bell pepper

1 cup fresh or frozen corn

2 cups cooked black beans

½ teaspoon ground cumin

1 teaspoon dried Mexican oregano

¼ cup chopped fresh cilantro

1. In the slow cooker, combine all the ingredients.

2. Cover and cook on low for 6 hours or on high for 3 hours.

3. Stir the soup and ladle it into bowls. Serve hot.

Ingredient Tip: Chayote is a pear-shaped, light green fruit with creamy white flesh. It is related to the cucumber, zucchini, and other members of the *Cucurbitaceae* family and has a very mild flavor. It was well-known to the Aztec and is considered by historians to be one of the first cultivated plants in the New World.

5

VEGETARIAN DISHES

≈≈≈≈≈≈≈≈≈≈≈≈≈≈≈≈

Mexican cuisine lends itself easily to both vegetarian and vegan recipes. Beans, rice, and corn are staple ingredients in Mexican culture as well as in vegetarian cookery. The spicy heat of various chiles, the warmth and earthiness of herbs and spices, and the zing of citrus give depth and flavor to vegetarian foods. As an added benefit, when you make your Mexican food favorites with vegetarian ingredients, the fat is reduced to almost nothing.

It's important to note that creamy, starchy foods soak up a lot of the heat from chiles and spices, so be especially careful to taste and adjust seasonings.

Canned or frozen foods can be substituted for the fresh ingredients in these recipes unless the instructions tell you otherwise. It's difficult to get flavorful tomatoes in January, for example; a good brand of diced tomatoes will work just fine instead. Cooked black beans, kidney beans, and pinto beans are interchangeable in most of the recipes that call for them.

CORN AND POBLANO PUDDING

Budín de Elote con Chile Poblano

SERVES 8 • PREP TIME: 15 MINUTES • COOK TIME: 3¼ HOURS (LOW)

❦ *This corn pudding is a filling, satisfying comfort food that will remind you somewhat of tamales and somewhat of southern spoon bread. Serve it with cooked beans to make a complete protein. To kick up the heat, substitute a couple of jalapeños or serrano chiles for one of the poblano chiles.*

Cooking spray

½ cup whole milk

¼ cup yellow cornmeal

¼ cup all-purpose flour

2 tablespoons sugar

1 teaspoon baking powder

2 eggs, lightly beaten

6 poblano chiles, fire-roasted (see page 158) peeled, and seeded

3 tablespoons unsalted butter, melted

1 (8.25-ounce) can cream-style corn

2 cups fresh or frozen corn

½ cup grated pepper Jack cheese

1. Spray the slow cooker with cooking spray.

2. In a large bowl, whisk together the milk, cornmeal, flour, sugar, baking powder, and eggs until smooth. Stir in the poblano chiles, butter, corn, and cheese. Spoon the batter into the slow cooker.

3. Cover and cook on low for 3 hours, or until the pudding is set. Remove the lid and cook uncovered for 15 more minutes.

4. Serve hot.

Ingredient Tip: Always take a small taste of chiles so you know how hot they are. Two peppers from the same plant can have different heat levels. When you know how hot they are, adjust your recipe accordingly.

QUINOA AND BLACK BEANS
Quinoa con Frijoles Negros

SERVES 6 • PREP TIME: 5 MINUTES • COOK TIME: 10 HOURS (LOW), 5 HOURS (HIGH)

This blend of quinoa and black beans is somewhat like a thick soup or hearty stew. Everything except the herbs goes into the slow cooker at one time, so there is very little prep time. You don't even have to mince the garlic or jalapeños—just mash them into the stew or remove them before serving. If you'd like to make this more quickly, use canned black beans and cut your cooking time down to 6 hours on low or 3 hours on high, or until the quinoa is tender.

2 dried chipotles

1 pound dried black beans, rinsed

¾ cup uncooked quinoa, rinsed

2 large tomatoes, diced, or 1 (28-ounce) can fire-roasted diced tomatoes

1 medium onion, diced

1 garlic clove, minced

2 medium bell peppers (any color), seeded and diced

2 jalapeños, halved and seeded, optional

4 cups water

3 cups Vegetable Stock (see page 48)

2 teaspoons chili powder

1 teaspoon ground cumin

¼ cup chopped fresh cilantro

Sea salt

Chopped avocado and lime wedges, for garnish

1. In the slow cooker, combine all the ingredients except the chili powder, cumin, cilantro, salt, avocado, and lime.

2. Cover and cook on low for 10 hours or on high for 5 hours.

3. Stir in the chili powder, cumin, and cilantro. Taste and season with salt as needed.

4. Remove the chipotles, and top the quinoa and beans with chopped avocado and a squeeze of lime before serving.

Cooking Tip: Never add salt to beans while they are cooking. Always wait until they are thoroughly tender, and then taste and add the minimum amount of salt. When added early in cooking, salt toughens the beans, and they never get that tender mushiness that everyone loves.

BLACK BEAN AND SPINACH ENCHILADAS

Enchiladas de Frijol y Espinaca

SERVES 6 • PREP TIME: 15 MINUTES • COOK TIME: 6 HOURS (LOW), 3 HOURS (HIGH)

♥♥♥ *It can be tough to get kids to eat their vegetables, and green veggies in particular. These enchiladas make it easy by mixing spinach with beans, corn, onions, and cheese. The spinach adds color, flavor, and nutrition to this dish. The chipotles in adobo make it spicy. Dipping the tortillas in the hot enchilada sauce helps make them pliable and easier to roll. Rice is a perfect side dish with these enchiladas. To keep it healthy, resist the urge to add refried beans as a side dish and serve sliced pineapple instead.*

2 cups cooked black or pinto beans

2 cups chopped fresh spinach

2 cups fresh or frozen corn

1 medium onion, chopped

2 tablespoons chopped chipotles in adobo

1 teaspoon ground cumin

Sea salt

2½ cups Fire-Roasted Enchilada Sauce (see page 40)

12 corn tortillas

2 cups queso quesadilla or Monterey Jack cheese

Cooking spray

The Night Before

1. In a large bowl, combine the beans, spinach, corn, onion, chipotles in adobo, and cumin. Mix gently. Taste and add salt if needed.

2. In a large saucepan over medium heat, heat the enchilada sauce. Dip each tortilla in the sauce and lay it on a flat surface, then add 2 tablespoons of the bean mixture, sprinkle with the cheese, and roll it up. Cover the enchiladas and refrigerate overnight. Store the remaining enchilada sauce and cheese for use in the morning.

In the Morning

1. Spray the slow cooker with cooking spray. Lay the enchiladas seam-side down in the slow cooker. You can add more layers to the top if you can't fit them all in one layer.

2. Cover the enchiladas with the remaining enchilada sauce. Sprinkle any remaining cheese over top.

3. Cover and cook for 6 hours on low or 3 hours on high.

4. Serve the enchiladas hot from the slow cooker.

Ingredient Tip: Corn tortillas are always used for true Mexican enchiladas. They have more flavor and texture than flour tortillas do. You'll find corn tortillas in blue, white, or yellow. Any of the three can be used interchangeably. Experiment to see what you like best.

SOUTHWESTERN BLACK BEANS AND RICE

Arroz con Frijoles Negros

SERVES 6 ● PREP TIME: LESS THAN 5 MINUTES ●
COOK TIME: 8 HOURS (LOW), 4 HOURS (HIGH) , PLUS 10 MINUTES (LOW)

Beans and rice is a staple food in most Central and South American countries. Not only is it a delicious, healthy combination, but it is also very budget friendly. It can be dressed up in a variety of ways depending on what's available locally. Brown rice is important to this recipe because it takes longer to cook than yellow or white rice and therefore holds its shape instead of getting mushy. This dish is even better the day after cooking. Don't worry about leftovers—they will freeze well for up to 6 months. Serve with grilled pineapple or a fruit salad and some warm flour tortillas.

½ pound dried black beans, rinsed

1 cup uncooked brown rice

1 medium onion, chopped

2 jalapeños

4 cups Vegetable Stock (see page 48)

Juice of 1 lime

1 cup chopped fresh cilantro

2 large tomatoes, diced

3 cups fresh or frozen corn

8 ounces grated Cheddar cheese

Sea salt

1. In the slow cooker, combine the beans, rice, onion, jalapeños, and stock.

2. Cover and cook on low for 8 hours or on high for 4 hours.

3. Add the lime juice, cilantro, tomatoes, corn, and cheese. Stir gently and cook for 10 more minutes on low. Taste and add salt if necessary.

4. Ladle the beans and rice into bowls and serve hot.

VEGETABLE ENCHILADAS WITH SEASONED TOFU

Enchiladas de Verdura con Tofu Sazonado

SERVES 6 ● PREP TIME: 15 MINUTES, PLUS OVERNIGHT ● COOK TIME: 8 HOURS (LOW)

❦❦ *Prepare yourself for a "meaty" meat-free dish. Because the tofu absorbs the season-ing overnight, it's packed with flavor when it comes out of the slow cooker. Cooking on low heat ensures that the mushrooms get tender and that the cheese doesn't separate. Like many highly seasoned foods, these enchiladas are even better the second day. Don't freeze leftovers—the sour cream can get grainy.*

12 ounces firm tofu, drained, pressed, and cut into bite-size cubes

2 tablespoons Taco Seasoning Mix (see page 156)

2 poblano chiles, fire-roasted (see page 158), peeled, seeded, and chopped

1 pound portabello mushrooms, chopped

½ medium onion, chopped

1 teaspoon ground cumin

½ teaspoon sea salt

½ cup chopped fresh cilantro

½ cup Mexican crema or sour cream

1½ cups grated queso quesadilla or pepper Jack cheese, divided

Cooking spray

12 corn tortillas

1 cup Green Salsa (see page 153)

The Night Before

> In a large bowl, toss together the tofu and the taco seasoning until the tofu is covered on all sides. Use a little more seasoning if you need to. Cover the bowl and refrigerate overnight.

In the Morning

1. To the large bowl with the tofu, add the poblano, mushrooms, onion, cumin, salt, and cilantro. Gently stir in the crema and ½ cup of the cheese.

2. Spray the slow cooker with cooking spray.

Continued

3. Warm the tortillas in a dry skillet over medium heat. Add some of the filling to a tortilla, roll it up, and lay it seam-side down in the slow cooker. Repeat with the rest of the filling and tortillas.

4. Cover the enchiladas with the green salsa and top with the remaining 1 cup of cheese, and cook on low for 8 hours. Serve hot.

Ingredient Tip: Tofu is made from soy milk, very much like mozzarella cheese is made from cow's or buffalo's milk. An acid is added to the soy milk and the mixture is allowed to stand until a curd is formed—that's tofu. It comes in silken, soft, or firm varieties, but for most main dish recipes you'll want the firm type.

NO-CHEESE ENCHILADA CASSEROLE

Cacerola de Enchiladas Sin Queso

SERVES 6 ● PREP TIME: 10 MINUTES ● COOK TIME: 6 HOURS (LOW), 3½ HOURS (HIGH)

This vegan enchilada casserole comes together quickly, and you can vary the ingredients according to what's available at your farmers' market. Instead of zucchini, try broccoli, cauliflower, sweet potatoes, or whatever you like. Corn tortillas have the most flavor, but flour tortillas soften to an almost dumpling-like consistency. Either works well in this recipe. Round out your meal with sliced cucumbers in a zesty Italian dressing, rice, and something chocolaty for dessert. Freeze any leftovers and use them for another meal.

Cooking spray

2 zucchini, diced

1 medium onion, chopped

1½ medium jalapeños, seeded and
    chopped, or more as desired

2 cups fresh or frozen corn

2 pounds tempeh, chopped

½ cup chopped fresh cilantro

1 teaspoon ground cumin

1 teaspoon ancho chili powder

½ teaspoon garlic powder

½ cup sliced black olives

8 Roma tomatoes, chopped,
    or 1 (28-ounce) can diced
    fire-roasted tomatoes

6 blue corn or other corn tortillas

1. Spray the slow cooker with cooking spray.

2. In a large bowl, combine all the ingredients except the tortillas. Spoon a thin layer of the vegetable mixture on the bottom of the slow cooker. Cover the mixture with a layer of tortillas

3. Spoon a thicker layer of the vegetable mixture on the tortillas. Cover with another layer of tortillas and repeat until the ingredients are used up, ending with a layer of tortillas.

4. Cover and cook on low for 6 hours or on high for 3½ hours.

5. Cut the casserole into slices and serve hot.

Ingredient Tip: Tempeh is a soy product made from cooked fermented soybeans and formed into a rectangle. Many manufacturers add whole grains, spices, and other ingredients to give it unique flavor. It has a texture similar to cooked hamburger and a nutty, meaty flavor.

LENTIL AND QUINOA TACOS

Tacos de Lentejas y Quinoa

SERVES 6 · PREP TIME: 5 MINUTES · COOK TIME: 10 HOURS (LOW), 5 HOURS (HIGH)

Lentils cook more quickly than dried beans and have plenty of protein and flavor. They come in several colors, but the flavors are much the same, so choose whichever one you prefer visually. Always rinse and pick through dried beans and lentils before cooking. There are sometimes stray clumps of dirt or tiny pebbles in with them. These tacos are smoky, spicy, and filling. They are also easy on the budget and the waistline—this recipe has almost no fat unless you add cheese. The toppings listed are only suggestions. You can add anything you like.

1½ cups red lentils

1½ cups quinoa

6 cups Vegetable Stock (see page 48)

2 tablespoons chopped chipotles in adobo, or more as desired

1 teaspoon smoked paprika

1 tablespoon Taco Seasoning Mix (see page 156)

Whole-wheat tortillas

TOPPINGS

Baby spinach leaves

Chopped tomatoes

Chopped onions

Chopped fresh cilantro

Chopped jalapeños

Chopped lettuce

Grated cheese

Queso fresco

Salsa

1. In the slow cooker, combine all the taco ingredients except the tortillas and the toppings.

2. Cover and cook on low for 10 hours or on high for 5 hours.

3. Warm the tortillas in a dry skillet over medium heat. Fill the warm tortillas with the filling and top with your favorite ingredients. Fold in half to serve.

Ingredient Tip: Quinoa is an ancient food similar in many ways to wheat, although it is technically not a grain. It was well-known to the Aztec and other indigenous Central and South American peoples. It is one of the few vegetable-based foods that is a complete protein. It is gluten-free and has a pleasant nutty flavor.

ENCHILADA CASSEROLE WITH SWEET POTATOES AND BEANS

Enchiladas de Mole con Camote y Frijoles

SERVES 6 · PREP TIME: 5 MINUTES · COOK TIME: 8 HOURS (LOW), 4 HOURS (HIGH)

This dish has all the flavor of your favorite Mexican food combined with all the comfort-food appeal of a casserole or lasagna. Layers of complex mole sauce, tortillas, vegetables, and melted cheese cook slowly all day, filling your home with a mouthwatering aroma. You can save time by buying the mole sauce, but the commercial version is not nearly as good as homemade. Serve this unique no-roll enchilada bake with a salad and plenty of sangria. It's a meal that your guests won't soon forget.

Cooking spray

2 cups Poblano Mole (see page 149), ½ cup reserved

3 cups cooked beans (black, pinto, red, or a mixture)

2 cups fresh or frozen corn

1 cup diced sweet potato or winter squash

1 cup chopped onion

12 corn tortillas

2 cups grated queso quesadilla or Monterey Jack cheese, ½ cup reserved

½ cup chopped fresh cilantro

1. Spray the slow cooker with cooking spray.

2. In a large bowl, gently mix 1½ cups of the mole with the beans, corn, sweet potato, and onion.

3. In the slow cooker, spread a little of this mixture on the bottom. Top with a layer of tortillas. Spread a layer of vegetable mixture over the top. Next, sprinkle some of the cheese over the vegetables, followed by a sprinkling of cilantro. Repeat the layers until all the filling is used, ending with a layer of tortillas.

4. Spread the reserved ½ cup of mole on the tortillas and sprinkle with the reserved ½ cup of cheese.

5. Cover and cook on low for 8 hours or on high for 4 hours, and serve hot.

CHEESY CHILI

Chili con Queso

SERVES 8 * PREP TIME: LESS THAN 5 MINUTES *
COOK TIME: 8 HOURS (LOW), 4 HOURS (HIGH)

Here's a cheesy, spicy chili that you'll add to your collection of favorite recipes. You can use cooked dried beans in this, but it's best to use canned beans since there are so many different kinds. Chili beans are canned beans in a smoky sauce that add lots of flavor to this autumn favorite. Serve it up, steaming hot, in big bowls to enjoy during those Saturday football games. It's perfect for potlucks and tailgating parties, too. Make sure you have plenty of crispy tortilla chips and ice-cold beer on hand. The chili is also fabulous ladled over baked potatoes. Game day has never been better than this.

2 (15-ounce) cans chili beans
(don't drain)

1 (15-ounce) can black beans, drained
and rinsed

2 (15-ounce) cans kidney beans, drained
and rinsed

1 (15-ounce) can pinto beans, drained
and rinsed

2 (14.5-ounce) cans diced tomatoes
with chiles

1 dried chipotle

2 zucchini, chopped

2 medium onions, chopped

4 garlic cloves, minced

1 green bell pepper, seeded and chopped

¼ cup tomato paste

1 tablespoon chili powder

1 teaspoon ground cumin

3 cups grated Colby cheese

1. In the slow cooker, combine everything except the cheese.

2. Cover and cook on low for 8 hours or on high for 4 hours.

3. Remove the chipotle, and stir in the cheese until it melts.

4. Serve with tortilla chips.

POBLANO AND CHEESE CASSEROLE

Rajas con Queso

SERVES 4 • PREP TIME: 15 MINUTES • COOK TIME: 5 HOURS (LOW)

This recipe is best made in a smaller 3- to 4-quart slow cooker. Generous amounts of cheese are layered with rajas—poblano chile peppers—*and then covered with a custard mixture. It cooks on low heat until the custard is set. A layer of crispy breadcrumbs is added to the top at the very end for texture and crunch. This is not a spicy dish but rather a creamy, cheesy comfort food. When made in the slow cooker, this recipe is very similar to a quiche in texture, although it doesn't taste "eggy." The addition of the pepper Jack gives it a little kick, but you can substitute Monterey Jack cheese if you want it to be milder.*

8 ounces Colby cheese, grated

8 ounces pepper Jack cheese, grated

Cooking spray

4 poblano chiles, fire-roasted
   (see page 158), seeded, and cut
   into wide strips

4 eggs

¾ cup heavy cream

½ teaspoon sea salt

½ cup all-purpose flour

½ cup panko breadcrumbs

Salsa

Sour cream

1. In a medium bowl, combine the cheeses.

2. Spray the slow cooker with cooking spray. Place a layer of poblano strips on the bottom and cover with a layer of cheese. Repeat until you have three layers.

3. In a large bowl, whisk together the eggs, cream, salt, and flour. Pour the mixture over the chiles and cheese.

4. Cover and cook on low for 5 hours, or until cooked through.

5. Top with the breadcrumbs, and serve topped with salsa and a dollop of sour cream.

TEMPEH CARNITAS

Carnitas de Tempeh

SERVES 6 · PREP TIME: 5 MINUTES · COOK TIME: 6 HOURS (LOW), 3 HOURS (HIGH)

Carnitas *means "little meat," and it generally refers to a dish of slow-cooked pork, shredded and served in tortillas. Tempeh Carnitas is a savory, vegan copycat of the more traditional pork dish, but there is no flavor lost in the translation. The tempeh is cut into cubes and then simmered along with garlic and herbs in a spicy citrus sauce. The citrus brightens the dish while the chipotle adds a nice heat. Traditional carnitas are not cooked with chiles. Spiciness is added to taste in the form of salsa when made into tacos.*

Generally speaking, dried herbs and spices should be added at the end of the cooking time, but in this case, they are added in the beginning with the other ingredients. Always taste your dish before serving, and adjust the seasonings as needed.

Cooking spray

1½ pounds tempeh, cut into
    bite-size cubes

5 garlic cloves

1 teaspoon ground cumin

1 teaspoon dried oregano

½ teaspoon smoked paprika

1 teaspoon chipotle powder

½ teaspoon sea salt

¾ cup fresh orange juice

2 tablespoons fresh lime juice

3 tablespoons chopped chipotles
    in adobo

12 flour tortillas

TOPPINGS

1 medium onion, chopped

Salsa

1 cup chopped fresh cilantro

3 jalapeños, seeded and chopped

2 medium avocados, chopped

6 lime wedges

1. Spray the slow cooker with cooking spray. Add the tempeh, garlic, cumin, oregano, smoked paprika, chipotle powder, and salt.

2. In a medium bowl, mix together the orange juice, lime juice, and chipotles, mashing the chipotles into the liquids. Pour this mixture over the ingredients in the slow cooker.

3. Cover and cook on low for 6 hours or on high for 3 hours.

4. Warm the tortillas in a dry skillet over medium heat or in the microwave. Fill the warm tortillas with the filling and top with your favorite ingredients.

5. Serve with lime wedges to squeeze over the carnitas.

Ingredient Tip: Smoked paprika is the Spanish version of the more popular Hungarian paprika. It is darker than regular paprika and gives dishes a smoky flavor without being overpowering. It enhances whatever dish it is in with just enough smokiness to make you think the dish was cooked over a campfire.

6

SEAFOOD AND POULTRY DISHES

~~~~~~~~~~~~~~~~~~~~~~

The cuisines of Mexico vary due to different local ingredients, but the one common tie in all real Mexican food is the use of fresh ingredients. Since chickens are relatively inexpensive and easy to raise almost anywhere, they are the animal protein of choice in many regions of Mexico. In the towns that line the long coastline, however, people are more likely to choose fresh seafood. Shrimp, red snapper, and sea bass are a few of the many seafood varieties you'll see used in Mexican cuisine.

Making fish in your slow cooker can be done, but you will need to keep in mind that the cooking times are very short, usually no more than 2 hours. Alternatively, if you wish to cook the rest of the ingredients longer, you can add the fish during the last hour of cooking time.

Chicken, however, turns out great using the low-and-slow method. The long cooking time results in tender meat imbued with the flavor of various spices, herbs, and aromatics added to the pot.

VERACRUZ-STYLE TILAPIA

Tilapia a la Veracruzana

SERVES 6 • PREP TIME: 5 MINUTES • COOK TIME: 2 TO 4 HOURS (LOW)

Veracruz-style red snapper is considered one of the national dishes of Mexico. Tilapia is much less expensive than snapper and works perfectly in this recipe; however, you can certainly use red snapper if you prefer. Traditionally, pickled jalapeños or pickled chiles gueros would take the place of the pepperoncini, but they can be difficult to find. Garnish the plate with lime wedges to be squeezed over the fish and serve it with rice, a crisp salad, and plenty of warm tortillas. Sliced ice-cold melon is a refreshing way to finish the meal.

Cooking spray

6 tilapia fillets (about 6 ounces each)

1 tablespoon olive oil

¼ teaspoon sea salt

½ teaspoon freshly ground black pepper

2 large tomatoes, chopped

1 large onion, chopped

1 bell pepper (any color), seeded and thinly sliced

½ cup sliced pimento-stuffed green olives

4 garlic cloves, sliced

1 medium pepperoncino, seeded and diced

2 tablespoons drained capers

6 lime wedges

1. Spray the slow cooker with cooking spray.

2. Brush the tilapia fillets with olive oil and sprinkle them lightly with salt and pepper. Lay the fillets on the bottom of the slow cooker.

3. In a medium bowl, combine the tomatoes, onion, bell pepper, olives, garlic, pepperoncino, and capers. Then spoon this mixture over the fillets.

4. Cover and cook on low for 2 to 4 hours, or until a meat thermometer inserted in the fish reads 145°F.

5. Carefully remove the fillets to warm plates and spoon some of the vegetables and sauce over each before serving. Garnish with lime wedges.

Warning: Be careful. Fish cooks very quickly, and some varieties will fall apart when cooked in a slow cooker. This recipe works because tilapia is a firm-fleshed fish and you don't cook it very long at all.

WHITE FISH WITH CILANTRO, JALAPEÑO, AND LIME

Pescado con Cilantro, Jalapeño y Limón

SERVES 6 • PREP TIME: 5 MINUTES • COOK TIME: 2 HOURS (LOW)

This dish is full of fresh flavors and just a little bite from the jalapeños. If you find the lime juice is too tangy for your taste, try this with orange juice or a combination of different citrus juices. This dish does cook quickly—it's not one of those fix-it-and-forget-it recipes. Since it spends only 2 hours in the slow cooker, plan this for a day when you are going to be home. Sea bass, red snapper, and tilapia are all good choices for this dish.

1 tablespoon olive oil

6 sea bass (or other firm white fish) fillets

3 tablespoons unsalted butter, melted

¼ teaspoon sea salt

½ cup chopped fresh cilantro

Zest of 1 lime

¼ cup fresh lime juice

2 tablespoons chopped jalapeño

Lime wedges, for garnish

1. Rub the inside of the slow cooker with the olive oil.

2. Brush the fish lightly with the melted butter, sprinkle it with salt, and then place it in the bottom of the slow cooker.

3. In a medium bowl, combine the cilantro, lime zest, lime juice, and jalapeño and spoon the mixture over the fish.

4. Cover and cook on low for 2 hours, or until a meat thermometer inserted in the fish reads 145°F.

5. Garnish the fish with lime wedges and serve it with warm whole-wheat tortillas, rice, and a salad.

SPICY FISH TACOS

Tacos de Pescado

SERVES 6 · PREP TIME: 5 MINUTES · COOK TIME: 1½ HOURS (LOW)

News flash: The fish tacos you probably love aren't an authentic Mexican food; they were actually concocted by a California beach bum in the last 40 or 50 years. Our version includes tender white fish that has been slow cooked with taco seasoning, lime, poblano chiles, and cilantro and then spooned into warm blue corn tortillas and sprinkled with your favorite toppings—perfect for a casual summer party.

2 tablespoons olive oil, plus 1 tablespoon
    for greasing the slow cooker

1½ pounds tilapia or sea bass fillets

½ teaspoon sea salt

2 tablespoons Taco Seasoning Mix
    (see page 156)

Zest of 1 lime

2 tablespoons fresh lime juice

2 roasted poblano chiles, diced
    (see page 158)

2 garlic cloves, minced

½ cup chopped fresh cilantro

12 blue corn tortillas

TOPPINGS

Green Salsa (see page 153)
    or Pico de Gallo (see page 151)

3 cups shredded cabbage

2 avocados, diced

¾ cup chopped scallions

Lime wedges

1. Rub the inside of the slow cooker with 1 tablespoon of olive oil.

2. Season the fish with the salt and taco seasoning, and then place it in the slow cooker.

3. In a medium bowl, combine the 2 tablespoons of olive oil with the lime zest, lime juice, chiles, garlic, and cilantro. Pour this mixture over the fish fillets in the slow cooker.

4. Cover and cook on low for 1½ hours, or until a meat thermometer inserted in the fish reads 145°F.

5. Warm the tortillas in a dry skillet over medium heat. Break the fish apart and divide it among the warm tortillas.

6. Add salsa, cabbage, avocado, scallions, and a squeeze of lime to each taco. Serve with Cilantro and Lime Rice (see page 123).

GREEN CHILE AND CHICKEN ENCHILADA CASSEROLE

Caserola de Pollo con Chile Verde

SERVES 6 ◦ PREP TIME: 10 MINUTES ◦ COOK TIME: 8 HOURS (LOW), 4 HOURS (HIGH)

Green chiles, chicken, and corn tortillas are slow cooked with a creamy, tangy sauce for a family-friendly dish that will rarely leave you with any leftovers. Many recipes use canned cream soups, which can be high in sodium and made with artificial ingredients, but this one uses rich, natural cream cheese that melts and combines with the other ingredients to make a silky sauce. If you love cream cheese, feel free to add up to an extra 8 ounces of the stuff. If you do add more cream cheese, add more Green Salsa to keep everything in balance.

1½ pounds cooked boneless, skinless chicken breasts, shredded

8 ounces cream cheese, cut into 1-inch cubes

3 cups Chicken Stock (see page 46)

1½ cups fresh or frozen corn

2 medium poblano chiles, diced

½ medium onion, chopped

1 cup Green Salsa (see page 153)

½ cup grated Colby cheese, plus more as desired

1 teaspoon ground cumin

½ teaspoon smoked paprika

½ teaspoon garlic powder

12 corn tortillas, torn into bite-size pieces

1. In the slow cooker, combine all the ingredients, stirring gently to blend.

2. Cover and cook on low for 8 hours or on high for 4 hours.

3. Serve with an extra sprinkle of Colby cheese if desired.

Ingredient Variation: To add even more flavor to this dish, fire-roast the poblano chiles, corn, and onion (see page 158). Be sure to remove the outer skin from the onion before you char it. The fire-roasted vegetables will add a subtle, smoky flavor to the dish that is irresistible.

TEQUILA AND LIME CHICKEN TACOS

Relleno de Pollo con Limón y Tequila para Tacos

SERVES 6 • PREP TIME: 5 MINUTES • COOK TIME: 8 HOURS (LOW), 4 HOURS (HIGH)

❦❦❦ *This dish is made with chicken thighs, which have more flavor than chicken breasts, but you can substitute chicken breasts if you like. The meat needs to be raw for this dish so it can absorb more of the flavor as it cooks. Although the recipe calls for tequila, you can substitute beer, orange juice, or pineapple juice if you prefer. The liquid smoke is optional, but it does add a nice extra kick of smoky flavor. Serve this dish with rice, Classic Refried Beans (see page 125), and frozen margaritas or a frosty glass of beer.*

1½ pounds boneless, skinless
   chicken thighs

¾ cup tequila

¼ cup fresh lime juice

2 garlic cloves

2 tablespoons chopped chipotles
   in adobo

1 tablespoon chili powder

2 teaspoons liquid smoke (optional)

1 teaspoon ground cumin

1 teaspoon dried oregano

1 teaspoon ancho chile powder

½ teaspoon smoked paprika

12 corn tortillas

TOPPINGS

Chopped red onion

Chopped avocado

Chopped cilantro

Grated queso quesadilla cheese

Red Salsa (see page 41) or Pico de Gallo
   (see page 151)

6 lime wedges

1. In the slow cooker, combine all the ingredients except the tortillas and toppings.

2. Cover and cook on low for 8 hours or on high for 4 hours.

3. Transfer the chicken to a cutting board and shred it using two forks. Return the shredded chicken to the slow cooker and stir to blend.

4. Warm the tortillas in a dry skillet over medium heat and fill them with the chicken mixture. Serve with the toppings.

SALSA CHICKEN

Pollo en Salsa

SERVES 6 • PREP TIME: 2 MINUTES • COOK TIME: 8 HOURS (LOW), 4 HOURS (HIGH)

❦ *Salsa Chicken could not be easier. You put raw chicken breasts in the bottom of the slow cooker and add salsa. The heat of the salsa will determine the heat of the final dish. Let it cook until dinnertime, and you'll have the most tender, flavorful chicken that you've ever experienced. The acids in the salsa tenderize and flavor the meat. You can eat the chicken breasts whole with whatever side dishes you like, or you can shred them and put them in taco shells, either crispy or soft. This dish freezes and reheats very well.*

1½ pounds boneless, skinless
   chicken breasts

2½ cups Red Salsa (see page 41)
   or Green Salsa (see page 153)

1. In the slow cooker, place the chicken and pour the salsa over it.

2. Cover and cook on low for 8 hours or on high for 4 hours.

3. Serve hot.

SMOKY CHICKEN FAJITAS WITH JALAPEÑO

Fajitas de Pollo con Jalapeños Asados

SERVES 6 ° PREP TIME: 5 MINUTES ° COOK TIME: 8 HOURS (LOW), 4 HOURS (HIGH)

❦❦❦ Fajitas are a part of summer for many people, with the meat coming hot off the grill along with plenty of blackened onions and peppers to stuff into a tortilla. But what do you do in the winter, when the grill is covered with snow and ice and you are craving these smoky, charred flavors? As this recipe proves, all you really need is a slow cooker to re-create the smoky and spicy fajitas of summer, even on the coldest of days.

2 to 3 tablespoons Fajita Seasoning Mix (see page 157)

½ teaspoon ancho chili powder

1 pound boneless, skinless chicken breasts

1 medium onion, cut into rings

2 medium bell peppers (any color), cut into thin strips

3 jalapeños, fire-roasted (see page 158), skins removed, seeded, and cut into thin strips

1 tablespoon liquid smoke

6 flour tortillas

TOPPINGS

¾ cup grated Colby cheese

1 large tomato, chopped

¾ cup Guacamole (see page 148)

¾ cup Mexican crema or sour cream

6 lime wedges

1. In a large bowl, mix together the Fajita Seasoning and ancho chili powder. Add the chicken to the bowl and toss to coat evenly in the seasoning mixture.

2. In the slow cooker, place the chicken with the onion, bell peppers, and jalapeños on top.

3. Sprinkle the liquid smoke over the vegetables.

4. Cover and cook on low for 8 hours or on high for 4 hours.

5. Warm the tortillas in a dry skillet over medium heat. Serve the fajitas with the warm tortillas and toppings.

Diet Variation: If you are vegetarian, substitute 2 pounds of firm tofu for the chicken. Freezing the tofu before using it will change its texture, and it will become very "meaty." Tempeh is another good vegetarian substitute.

CILANTRO AND CITRUS CHICKEN

Pollo con Limón y Cilantro

SERVES 6 · PREP TIME: 15 MINUTES · COOK TIME: 8 HOURS (LOW), 4 HOURS (HIGH)

❦❦ *This is a spicy, tangy main dish that you can put together quickly and easily. The lime gives the meat a bright flavor as well as a delicate texture. Shred the meat and serve it in soft tortillas generously topped with your favorite ingredients. Or, if you prefer, serve it just as it comes out of the slow cooker. Round out your dinner with rice, a salad, and some grilled pineapple with a scoop of vanilla ice cream on top.*

½ cup fresh lime juice

2 teaspoons sea salt

1 teaspoon ancho chili powder

½ teaspoon freshly ground black pepper

2 garlic cloves, minced

6 boneless, skinless chicken breasts

2 cups cooked black beans

1 cup chopped fresh cilantro

1 cup fresh or frozen corn

½ medium red bell pepper, seeded and chopped

½ medium onion, chopped

1½ medium (or 1 large) jalapeños, seeded and chopped

½ cup Chicken Stock (see page 46)

1. In the slow cooker, add all of the ingredients.

2. Cover and cook on low for 8 hours or on high for 4 hours.

3. Serve hot.

Time-saving Tip: This recipe is very quick and easy to make, but you can make it even faster. Put all the ingredients in a large freezer bag, push the air out, seal it, and freeze it. When you are ready to cook, thaw the bag out in the refrigerator overnight and then dump the contents in the slow cooker. It can be frozen for up to 3 months.

CHICKEN MOLE

Pollo con Mole

SERVES 6 · PREP TIME: 10 MINUTES, PLUS SOAKING TIME ·
COOK TIME: 8 HOURS (LOW), 4 HOURS (HIGH)

If you like exotically flavored foods, then this slow-cooked chicken mole is a must-try. Boneless, skinless chicken breast is slowly cooked in a complex tomato-based sauce that is spicy and full of flavor. With three kinds of chiles, a generous amount of Mexican chocolate, and lots of warm spices, this dish will have your neighbors knocking at the door with forks and plates in hand. Can't find the mulato chile? It's fine to leave it out.

1 dried mulato chile

2 dried ancho chiles

2 pounds boneless, skinless
   chicken breasts

Sea salt

½ teaspoon freshly ground black pepper,
   plus more as needed

1 (28-ounce) can diced fire-roasted
   tomatoes

1 medium onion, chopped

2 chipotles in adobo sauce

1 cup sliced almonds

¼ cup raisins

3 ounces chopped Mexican chocolate or
   bittersweet chocolate

3 garlic cloves

1 teaspoon ground cumin

½ teaspoon ground roasted cinnamon

½ teaspoon ground aniseed

¼ teaspoon ground cloves

Chopped fresh cilantro for garnish

The Night Before

In a medium glass bowl, place the dried chiles and add warm water until they are just covered. Let the chiles soak overnight at room temperature.

In the Morning

1. Season the chicken with salt and pepper to taste and place it in the slow cooker.

2. In a blender, combine the remaining ingredients, except the cilantro, and process until smooth. Pour this mixture over the chicken.

3. Cover and cook on low for 8 hours or on high for 4 hours.

4. Serve hot with chopped fresh cilantro sprinkled over the top.

CHICKEN AND MANGO TINGA

Tinga de Pollo con Mango

SERVES 6 • PREP TIME: 10 MINUTES • COOK TIME: 6 HOURS (LOW), 3 HOURS (HIGH)

Piquant and sweet, this tinga is an intriguing twist on a classic Mexican dish. Although this recipe isn't terribly spicy, it does warm your taste buds with several waves of flavor—first from the fresh ginger, then from the jalapeños, and finally from the smoky chipotle. Canned fire-roasted tomatoes are used here because they give a deeper flavor to the dish than fresh tomatoes can. Serve the chicken with rice: Put a scoop of rice in a bowl, add a scoop of chicken, and then ladle the sauce over the top. Don't forget a squeeze of lime.

1 medium bell pepper (any color), diced

1 medium onion, chopped

1 medium mango, chopped

2 pounds boneless, skinless chicken breast

2 medium jalapeños, chopped

3 garlic cloves, minced

1½ teaspoons chipotle chili powder

1 tablespoon grated fresh ginger or
   1 teaspoon dried ginger

1 teaspoon sea salt

½ teaspoon ground cumin

¼ teaspoon ground roasted cinnamon

1 (14.5-ounce) can fire-roasted tomatoes

1 cup Chicken Stock (see page 46)

1 cup mango nectar

6 lime wedges, for garnish

1. In the slow cooker, combine the bell pepper, onion, and mango, and then place the chicken breast on top.

2. In a medium bowl, combine the jalapeños, garlic, spices, tomatoes, chicken stock, and mango nectar, and pour this mixture over the chicken.

3. Cover and cook on low for 6 hours or on high for 3 hours. Serve hot, garnished with the lime wedges.

Ingredient Tip: Fire-roasted tomatoes are available canned, but it's easy to make your own. Cut ripe tomatoes in half (leave the skins on) and lay them cut-side down on a baking sheet. Heat the broiler to the highest heat and put the tomatoes under it for 5 to 10 minutes, or until the skin blackens and is blistered. Let cool and remove the skins or not, as desired.

THREE-SPICE MEXICAN CHICKEN AND RICE

Arroz con Pollo a las Tres Especias

SERVES 6 ∘ PREP TIME: 5 MINUTES ∘ COOK TIME: 8 HOURS (LOW), 4 HOURS (HIGH)

Chicken and rice is a classic dish in almost every cuisine in the world, and for good reason. It's inexpensive, easy to make, filling, and delicious. This south-of-the-border version contains generous amounts of spices: warm, earthy cumin; smoky paprika; and chipotle. Keep in mind that rice will cut down on the spiciness of the chiles, so add more chipotle powder and jalapeños if you like your food at a four-alarm level. Using converted rice instead of the conventional kind means that the rice will be tender and perfect at the end of the cooking time. Conventional rice may not cook fast enough, and instant rice is likely to disintegrate into a gummy paste that's not very appealing.

Cooking spray

3 cups Chicken Stock (see page 46)

1½ cups uncooked converted rice (not instant)

1½ cups Red Salsa (see page 41) or Green Salsa (see page 153)

1 tablespoon Taco Seasoning Mix (see page 156)

½ teaspoon chipotle powder

½ teaspoon ground cumin

½ teaspoon smoked paprika

1½ pounds boneless, skinless chicken thighs

1 medium onion, chopped

1 cup cooked kidney beans

½ cup fresh or frozen corn

4 jalapeños, seeded and chopped

½ cup chopped fresh cilantro

1. Spray the slow cooker with cooking spray. Add the chicken stock, rice, salsa, taco seasoning, chipotle powder, cumin, and smoked paprika, stirring gently to mix. Add the chicken, onion, beans, corn, and jalapeños.

2. Cover and cook for 8 hours on low or 4 hours on high.

3. Transfer the chicken to a cutting board and chop it into bite-size pieces, then return it to the slow cooker. Stir in the cilantro, and serve.

CHICKEN BURRITOS SUIZA

Burritos de Pollo a la Suiza

SERVES 6 • PREP TIME: 10 MINUTES • COOK TIME: 4 HOURS (LOW), 2 HOURS (HIGH)

❦ OR ❦❦❦ *Suiza means "in the Swiss style" and reflects the influence of international cuisine on Mexican foods. This is a rich, creamy dish that is either somewhat spicy or call-the-fire-department hot, depending on whether you use the pepper Jack or habanero Jack cheese. If you don't want it to have any heat, use plain Monterey Jack. That will keep it mild enough for the kids, and those who want more heat can add a spicier cheese, salsa, or sliced jalapeños to their burritos. Burritos are a meal all by themselves, but to round them out nutritionally, serve them with sliced cucumbers that have marinated for 30 minutes or so in vinaigrette or Italian dressing.*

1 cup Chicken Stock (see page 46)

6 ounces cream cheese, cut into 1-inch cubes

4 cups cooked, diced chicken breast

2 garlic cloves, chopped

½ cup sliced jalapeños (optional)

1 cup Mexican crema or sour cream

2 cups grated pepper Jack or habanero Jack cheese, divided

Cooking spray

6 flour tortillas, burrito size

6 tablespoons sliced black olives

1. In a large microwave-safe bowl, combine the chicken stock and cream cheese. Cover the bowl, and microwave on high until the cream cheese is very soft and can be whisked into the stock smoothly.

2. Add the chicken breast, garlic, jalapeños (if using), crema, and half the grated cheese to the cream cheese mixture. Stir until well mixed.

3. Spray the inside of the slow cooker with cooking spray. Transfer the mixture to the slow cooker.

4. Cover and cook on low for 4 hours or on high for 2 hours.

5. Warm the tortillas in a dry skillet over medium heat. Fill the warmed tortillas with the chicken mixture and top with the black olives and remaining cheese. To secure the burritos, fold the bottom of each filled tortilla up about 1 inch. Fold one side over to cover the filling and then roll to enclose it completely. Repeat with the remaining tortillas and filling.

6. Serve with your favorite salsa on the side.

TAMALE CASSEROLE

Cacerola Estilo Tamales

~~~~~~~~

SERVES 6 · PREP TIME: 15 MINUTES · COOK TIME: 6 HOURS (LOW), 3 HOURS (HIGH)

Tamales are a favorite Mexican food for most people, but they can be time consuming and difficult to make for the inexperienced cook. This tamale casserole is quick and easy, and it gives you all the flavors of freshly made tamales. You can make the topping using any of your favorite cornbread recipes or keep it easy with a mix from the store. Although this recipe calls for cooked ground turkey, you can use shredded cooked chicken, cooked ground pork, cooked ground beef, or a combination. In fact, you can even make it completely vegetarian by using all beans.

Cooking spray

1 pound lean ground turkey, cooked

1 poblano chile, fire-roasted, peeled, seeded, and chopped (see page 158)

4 scallions, chopped

3 cups cooked black beans

2 cups fresh or frozen corn

1 large tomato, diced

½ cup chopped fresh cilantro

¼ cup sliced black olives

1 cup Fire-Roasted Enchilada Sauce (see page 40)

1 teaspoon ground cumin

½ teaspoon chili powder

¼ teaspoon freshly ground black pepper

1 (8.5-ounce) package cornbread mix

1 cup grated Colby cheese

1. Spray the slow cooker with cooking spray.

2. In a large bowl, mix the turkey, poblano chile, scallions, black beans, corn, tomatoes, cilantro, and olives.

3. In a medium bowl, mix together the enchilada sauce, cumin, chili powder, and black pepper, and pour it over the meat and bean mixture, stirring gently to mix. Spoon the mixture into the slow cooker.

4. Make the cornbread batter according to the recipe or package instructions, but do not bake it. Spoon the cornbread batter over the meat and bean mixture in the slow cooker. Sprinkle the cheese on top.

5. Cover and cook on low for 6 hours or on high for 3 hours, or until the cornbread springs back to the touch.

6. Slice the casserole and serve hot.

Ingredient Tip: If you'd like to save time, you can buy ready-made polenta. It comes in tubes, and you can cut it into 1-inch slices and lay them over the filling instead of using cornbread. You can usually find the tubes in the baking section of your grocery store.

TURKEY MOLE

Pavo en Mole

SERVES 6 ∘ PREP TIME: 20 MINUTES, PLUS OVERNIGHT ∘ COOK TIME: 10 HOURS (LOW)

❦❦❦ *Anyone who has seen the movie* Like Water for Chocolate *will likely remember the sensual scene where Tita is grinding ingredients for turkey mole in a molcajete and Pedro comes in to gaze at her with deep longing on his face. Well, you might not get looks of longing when you fix this easy Turkey Mole, although you will likely get looks of sincere appreciation. This recipe is just that good. If you have a molcajete, use it for grinding the nuts, seeds, and chiles. If not, a blender will work just fine. It might seem like a complicated recipe, but it looks much more difficult and time consuming than it really is.*

½ cup smoked almonds

¼ cup sesame seeds

¼ cup peanuts

1 dried mulato chile, seeded
    (seeds reserved)

3 dried pasilla chiles, seeded
    (seeds reserved)

3 dried ancho chiles, seeded
    (seeds reserved)

1 teaspoon ground roasted cinnamon

½ teaspoon ground aniseed

½ teaspoon freshly ground black pepper

¼ teaspoon ground cloves

2 cups turkey or Chicken Stock (page 46)

¼ cup fruity red wine

½ cup panko breadcrumbs

½ medium onion, chopped

5 garlic cloves

2 ounces Mexican chocolate or bittersweet
    chocolate, chopped

1 tablespoon sugar

Cooking spray

1 (3-pound) boneless, skinless turkey breast

The Night Before

1. On a comal or in heavy griddle or heavy stainless steel skillet over medium-high heat, toast the almonds, sesame seeds, peanuts, and seeds from the dried chiles for about 5 minutes. Remove the mixture from the griddle.

2. Toast the chiles lightly on the griddle for about 1 minute on each side.

3. In a molcajete or blender, grind the chiles, seeds, and nuts. Stir in the cinnamon, aniseed, black pepper, and cloves.

4. Transfer the mixture to an airtight container and leave it out overnight at room temperature.

In the Morning

1. In a medium bowl, whisk the chile and nut mixture with the turkey stock.

2. Add the wine to the stock, and then stir in the breadcrumbs, onion, garlic, chocolate, and sugar.

3. Spray a slow cooker with cooking spray.

4. In the slow cooker, place the turkey breast and pour the stock mixture over it.

5. Cover and cook on low for 10 hours.

6. Serve the turkey sliced or shredded with warm tortillas, rice, or Corn on the Cob with Chili and Lime (see page 122).

7

MEAT DISHES

~~~~~~~~~~~~~~~~~~~~

Think of your favorite Mexican foods, and you will likely envision things like beef *barbacoa*, tacos, and savory pork roasts. While fish and seafood dishes developed on the coasts and chicken was the primary ingredient in the central and southern regions of Mexico, pork, beef, goat, and lamb were very common in northern and central Mexico. It was these areas that the European explorers found to be perfect for raising cattle, goats, and sheep. Many of the traditional dishes of Mexico rely on these meats, either simmered slowly in huge pots or grilled over open fires.

These meats adapt well to slow cooking. They are cooked until tender and then spooned into tacos, burritos, or enchiladas, or simply served with rice to soak up the savory sauces. These hearty meats stand up to strong flavors, so don't be shy with the chiles and spices.

Inexpensive, less tender cuts of meat are perfect for these recipes because the acids from tomatoes and sauces break down and tenderize the meat during the long, slow cooking time. As a general rule, the tougher the cut, the longer the cooking time and the lower the temperature should be.

SMOKY CHIPOTLE AND BEEF TACOS

Tacos de Res en Chipotle

SERVES 6 · PREP TIME: 10 MINUTES · COOK TIME: 8 HOURS (LOW), 4½ HOURS (HIGH)

❦❦ *Beef tacos are classic Mexican street food. Tacos are rarely the main meal in Mexico, but they are typically enjoyed as a quick meal before midday or a snack later in the evening. Soft corn tortillas are most commonly used, but soft flour tortillas can be used as well. The long, slow cooking time called for in this recipe results in tender meat, spicy with chipotle and ancho chile flavors. The roasted cinnamon adds a bit of warm spice. Toppings can include grated cheese, lettuce, chopped tomatoes, diced avocados, or almost anything else you can think of. Pile on your favorites.*

1 tablespoon chili powder

1½ teaspoons sea salt

1 teaspoon ground cumin

1 teaspoon ancho chili powder

½ teaspoon smoked paprika

½ teaspoon ground roasted cinnamon

2 pounds lean boneless beef chuck roast

1 medium onion, diced

6 garlic cloves, minced

1 cup Beef Stock (see page 47)

2 tablespoons tomato paste

2 chipotles in adobo, minced

12 flour tortillas

1. In a small bowl, combine the chili powder, salt, cumin, ancho chili powder, smoked paprika, and roasted cinnamon. Rub the seasoning mixture on all sides of the beef.

2. Place the beef in the slow cooker and top it with the onion and garlic.

3. In a medium bowl, whisk together the beef stock, tomato paste, and minced chipotle. Pour this mixture over the beef

4. Cover and cook on low for 8 hours or on high for 4½ hours.

5. Shred the meat using two forks, and serve the meat in the flour tortillas with your favorite toppings.

Time-saving Tip: Almost all beef can be improved by taking the time to sear or char the meat on all sides before putting it in the slow cooker. When you don't have the time but you want that flavor, add a tablespoon or so of liquid smoke.

TENDER BEER-BRAISED BEEF FAJITAS

Fajitas de Res a la Cerveza

SERVES 6 • PREP TIME: 5 MINUTES • COOK TIME: 10 HOURS (LOW), 6 HOURS (HIGH)

Tender beef, spicy peppers, and onions—who can resist a smoking plate of fajitas? You can make this version any time of the year because the slow cooker does all the work. In fact, you may find that you prefer the slow-cooked version, since it is often more tender than the traditional grilled version. Pile warm flour tortillas high with meat, onions, peppers, grated cheese, and guacamole or sour cream (or both). There's nothing like it. Fajitas aren't actually Mexican at all. They became popular on the ranches in West Texas in the 1930s. The parts of the cow that the rancher didn't want, such as the offal, head, and skirt steak, were given to the Mexican ranch hands, who turned the "waste" into dishes that are found in many restaurants today.

2 tablespoons Fajita Seasoning Mix
   (see page 157)

1½ pounds flank steak

Cooking spray

4 poblano chiles, seeded and
   cut into strips

1 medium onion, sliced

1 teaspoon liquid smoke (optional)

¼ cup beer

12 flour tortillas

TOPPINGS

Grated cheese

Sour cream

Guacamole (see page 148)

1. Rub the Fajita Seasoning into the meat on all sides. Set the meat aside.

2. Spray the slow cooker with cooking spray. Place half of the onion slices on the bottom, and then place the meat on top of them. Layer the chiles and remaining onion on top of the meat.

3. Pour the liquid smoke (if using) and the beer into the cooker.

4. Cover and cook on low for 10 hours or on high for 6 hours, until the meat can be shredded easily with two forks.

5. Shred the meat, then spoon it into tortillas and top with your favorite toppings.

BEEF BARBACOA

Barbacoa de Res

SERVES 6 · PREP TIME: 5 MINUTES · COOK TIME: 10 HOURS (LOW)

🍴🍴🍴 Barbacoa *is a slow-cooked dish that can be made with any meat, including venison, buffalo, goat, or mutton. Here it's made with beef and, specifically, a bone-in roast to add a lot of flavor to the dish. The several types of chiles used in this recipe give it heat. It is not for the faint of heart.*

3 pounds lean, bone-in beef roast

2 tablespoons apple cider vinegar

2 tablespoons fresh lime juice

1 dried chipotle

1 dried mulato chile

2 dried guajillo chiles

1 chipotle in adobo, chopped

1 tablespoon adobo sauce from the can

1 medium onion, diced

2 teaspoons ground cumin

2 teaspoons dried Mexican oregano

1 teaspoon sea salt

½ teaspoon garlic powder

½ teaspoon ground roasted cinnamon

1 cup Beef Stock (see page 47), beer, or water

1. In the slow cooker, combine all the ingredients. Cove and cook on low heat for 10 hours, or until the beef is very tender.

2. Transfer the beef to a cutting board; remove the bones and shred the meat using two forks.

3. Place the shredded meat in a serving bowl and add some of the cooking liquid to moisten it.

4. Taste and adjust the seasonings. Serve warm.

Recipe Variation: Barbacoa can be served in burritos or tacos with any of the toppings you love. It can also be made into another common Mexican street food called a *torta*. This is a roll split and filled with barbacoa or other filling.

MARINATED BRAISED BEEF BURRITOS

Burritos de Carne Deshebrada

SERVES 6 ● PREP TIME: 20 MINUTES, PLUS OVERNIGHT ● COOK TIME: 10 HOURS (LOW)

❦ *This is a version of* carne deshebrada, *a slowly simmered beef dish resulting in tender, highly seasoned meat that can be used in tacos, tortas, tostadas, or whatever you like. Here it is the filling for burritos, overflowing with meat, cheese, crema, and salsa. These burritos make a filling lunch or casual dinner. This recipe makes a lot of shredded beef. Divide up leftovers into recipe-size portions and put them into freezer containers along with some of the liquid from the slow cooker. You'll be able to have a mouthwatering Mexican meal at a moment's notice.*

FOR THE MARINADE

½ cup olive oil

¼ cup fresh lime juice

1 tablespoon Worcestershire sauce

1 tablespoon soy sauce

1 teaspoon hot sauce

½ teaspoon ground cumin

3 garlic cloves, minced

1 serrano chile, seeded and minced

FOR THE BEEF

3 pounds beef brisket, fat trimmed, cut into 1-pound pieces

3 tablespoons olive oil

2 medium onions, diced

1 cup Beef Stock (see page 47)

1 medium red bell pepper, seeded and diced

2 serrano chiles, seeded and minced

½ teaspoon dried Mexican oregano

1 teaspoon garlic powder

1 (28-ounce) can diced fire-roasted tomatoes

FOR THE BURRITOS

6 burrito-size flour tortillas

1 cup grated queso fresco or Monterey Jack cheese

1 cup Mexican crema or sour cream

1 cup Red Salsa (see page 41) or Green Salsa (see page 153)

The Night Before

1. In a large bowl, combine the marinade ingredients.

2. Place the brisket pieces in a resealable bag and cover them with the marinade. Seal the bag and refrigerate it overnight.

Continued

In the Morning

1. In the bottom of the slow cooker, combine the olive oil, onions, beef stock, bell pepper, serrano chiles, oregano, garlic powder, and tomatoes, stirring gently to mix.

2. Remove the meat from the resealable bag and discard the marinade. Place the meat in the slow cooker on top of the tomato mixture, and cook on low for 10 hours.

3. Transfer the beef to a cutting board and shred it using two forks. Return the shredded beef to the slow cooker and stir it into the sauce.

To Assemble the Burritos

1. Warm the tortillas in a dry skillet over medium-high heat.

2. Put some of the beef down the middle of each tortilla. Top with cheese, crema, and salsa.

3. Fold the bottom of each filled tortilla up about an inch and then roll from the side.

4. Serve hot.

Ingredient Tip: How do you choose a good beef brisket? For the most savings, choose a large, untrimmed brisket in Cryovac packaging. Try to bend the package and make the ends come together. The closer you can get them, the more tender the meat is.

CHIPOTLE BEEF AND POBLANO STEW

Guisado de Res con Chipotle y Poblano

SERVES 6 • PREP TIME: 5 MINUTES • COOK TIME: 10 HOURS (LOW), 5 HOURS (HIGH)

Stews are served in nearly every Mexican kitchen, and every cook has his or her own version that utilizes favorite flavors and seasonal ingredients. In that tradition, plan on using this recipe as a foundation for your own interpretation. Beef stew meat absorbs the flavor from chipotles, poblanos, onions, and garlic in this recipe. It cooks until it is fork tender and a little spicy. If you like it less spicy, cut back on the chipotle. Put the toppings in individual bowls on the table so everyone can top their stew with the things they like best.

2 cups fresh or frozen corn

1½ pounds lean beef stew meat

2 chipotles in adobo, chopped

2 medium onions, chopped

2 poblano chiles, seeded and diced

3 garlic cloves, chopped

3 large tomatoes, diced, or
    2 (14.5-ounce) cans diced tomatoes

1 teaspoon ground cumin

½ teaspoon sea salt

½ teaspoon freshly ground black pepper

TOPPINGS

1 avocado, diced

Chopped fresh cilantro

6 tablespoons sour cream

Tortilla chips

1. In the slow cooker, combine all the ingredients, except the toppings, and cook on low for 10 hours or on high for 5 hours.

2. Serve the stew in bowls topped with avocado, cilantro, and sour cream, with tortilla chips on the side.

   Ingredient Tip: It can be tricky to tell if an avocado is ripe. Hold it in the palm of your hand and gently squeeze the bottom. If it yields to firm pressure but does not feel too soft, then it should be just right.

BEEF STEW WITH POTATOES

Carne Guisada con Papas

SERVES 6 • PREP TIME: 10 MINUTES • COOK TIME: 6 TO 8 HOURS ON LOW

A Tex-Mex restaurant staple, carne guisada, or beef stew, can be made with countless variations. Here the meat is slow cooked in a seasoned beef broth until it is so tender that it's falling apart. While you don't have to brown the beef in this dish, taking a few minutes to brown it in a hot oiled pan will yield a more appealing color and a richer flavor. Don't be afraid to adjust this recipe to suit your family's preferences—add corn, carrots, or any other vegetables that you happen to have on hand.

1 teaspoon salt

1 teaspoon ground black pepper

1 teaspoon chili powder

½ teaspoon ground cumin

2 pounds beef stew meat

3 jalapeños, seeded and chopped

1 large onion, chopped

1 bell pepper, seeded and chopped

3 or 4 garlic cloves, minced

3 large baking potatoes, cubed

1 (14.5-ounce) can diced tomatoes
   with chiles

3 cups beef stock

½ cup red wine

½ cup water

The Night Before

> In a small bowl, mix the salt, pepper, chili powder, and cumin. Place the beef in a storage container, and then sprinkle the spice mixture over it. Seal the container and refrigerate it overnight.

In the Morning

1. To the slow cooker, add the seasoned beef and the rest of the ingredients.

2. Cook on low for 6 to 8 hours, or until the potatoes are tender.

3. Serve warm.

> **Ingredient Substitution:** Pork works just as well as beef in this recipe. Cut a pork roast into cubes about the size of stew meat and follow the recipe as written. The pork comes out tender and flavorful. You can also use a beef or pork roast without cutting it into cubes—just adjust the cook time to 8 to 10 hours.

RED CHILI WITH QUESO FRESCO

Chili Colorado con Queso Fresco

SERVES 6 • PREP TIME: 10 MINUTES • COOK TIME: 8 HOURS (LOW), 4 HOURS (HIGH)

❦❦ *Red chili, also called Chili Colorado, has nothing to do with the state of Colorado but refers to the red color of the chili itself. Layers of flavor are built by the variety of chiles that go into this dish. You can easily vary the flavor or douse the heat by substituting other varieties of chiles for those listed. There are no tomatoes in this dish. The flavor is purely from the chiles, herbs, and spices. When the meat is cooked, shred it with two forks and add it to bowls. Top with a little cheese and serve it with tortilla chips. This chili freezes well, but you aren't likely to have any leftovers to worry about.*

1 dried pasilla chile, seeded and diced

1 dried guajillo chile, seeded and diced

1 dried chipotle chile, seeded and diced

1 dried mulato chile, seeded and diced

1 medium onion, diced

2 garlic cloves, minced

½ medium red bell pepper, seeded and chopped

2 jalapeños

1 medium poblano chile, seeded and diced

1 teaspoon dried Mexican oregano

1 teaspoon chili powder

½ teaspoon ground cumin

½ teaspoon smoked paprika

½ teaspoon ground roasted cinnamon

Cooking spray

2 pounds lean, boneless beef roast

6 tablespoons grated queso fresco or Monterey Jack cheese

The Night Before

In a small bowl, pour in hot water over the pasilla, guajillo, chipotle, and mulato chiles just to cover them, and let them soak overnight at room temperature.

In the Morning

1. In a blender, add the chiles and soaking water and the remaining ingredients, except the meat and cheese, and blend until smooth.

2. Spray a slow cooker with cooking spray.

Continued

3. In the slow cooker, place the beef and pour the chile mixture over the top. Cook on low for 8 hours or on high for 4 hours.

4. Transfer the beef to a cutting board and shred it using two forks, then return the shredded beef to the slow cooker and stir it into the chili.

5. Serve the chili sprinkled with cheese.

Ingredient Variation: Chili Colorado is delicious as is, but you can also use it for enchiladas. Just spoon it into corn tortillas, roll them tightly, and place them seam-side down in a greased baking dish. Cover with Fire-Roasted Enchilada Sauce (see page 40) and grated cheese, and then bake for 20 minutes at 375°F.

THREE-ALARM RED CHILI BURRITOS

Burritos de Chili Picoso

SERVES 6 • PREP TIME: 5 MINUTES • COOK TIME: 10 HOURS (LOW), 5 HOURS (HIGH)

🌶🌶🌶 *This simple version of red chili isn't quite as hot or complex as the recipe on page 103, but it is quick and easy. The spicy heat found in this burrito is from the chipotle Jack cheese. If you want it spicier, use habanero Jack. For less heat, go with pepper Jack or plain Monterey Jack cheese. These burritos are especially good if you happen to have some leftover Cheese Dip with Meat (see page 36). Heat the Cheese Dip with Meat up and spoon it over the burritos. You'll have to eat it with a knife and fork, but it's worth it.*

1½ pounds lean beef chuck

1½ cups Fire-Roasted Enchilada Sauce
(see page 40)

2 cups Classic Refried Beans
(see page 125)

6 burrito-size flour tortillas

1½ cups grated chipotle Jack cheese

1. In the slow cooker, combine the meat and enchilada sauce, and cook on low for 10 hours or on high for 5 hours.

2. Transfer the beef to a cutting board and shred it using two forks, then return the shredded beef to the slow cooker and stir it into the sauce.

3. Warm the refried beans in a small saucepan over medium heat.

4. Warm the tortillas in a dry skillet over medium-high heat.

5. Put about 2 tablespoons of the beans down the center of each tortilla. Spoon a generous amount of the meat on top. Cover with a generous amount of cheese. Fold the bottom of each tortilla up and roll tightly.

6. Serve hot.

BEEF AND POBLANO TAMALE PIE

Budín de Tamal de Res y Chile Poblano

SERVES 6 • PREP TIME: 15 MINUTES • COOK TIME: 5 HOURS (LOW), 2½ HOURS (HIGH)

Tamale pie gives you the flavor of tamales without the work. While most tamale pies have a cornmeal topping, this one is made in layers with corn tortillas separating each layer. As they cook, the tortillas get soft, and everything combines to make a kid-friendly, comfort-food dinner that is deceptively easy. Because the cooking time on low is still only 5 hours, it's important to pre-cook the meat rather than place it in the slow cooker uncooked. With this extra time and the relatively short cooking time, you may want to save this recipe for a weekend day when you have more flexibility in your schedule. If you'd like to cut back on the meat, add a cup or two of cooked kidney beans, black beans, or pinto beans and use half the amount of meat.

Cooking spray

1½ pounds lean ground beef

1 medium onion, chopped

½ medium poblano chile, seeded
  and chopped

1 cup fresh or frozen corn

1 cup Fire-Roasted Enchilada Sauce
  (see page 40)

9 corn tortillas

1½ cups grated Colby cheese

1. Spray the slow cooker with cooking spray.

2. In a large skillet over medium-high heat, cook the ground beef, onion, and poblano until the meat is no longer pink, 4 to 6 minutes. Drain off the fat and blot the meat with paper towels.

3. Add the corn and enchilada sauce to the skillet and mix well.

4. Place 3 tortillas, overlapping, on the bottom of the slow cooker. Cover with one-third of the meat and one-third of the cheese. Repeat the layers twice more, leaving off the cheese on the last layer. Cook on low for 5 hours or on high for 2½ hours.

5. Top with the remaining cheese, cover the slow cooker, and turn off the heat. Serve when the cheese is melted.

TAQUERIA-STYLE SHREDDED BEEF SOFT TACOS

Tacos de Carne Deshebrada Estilo Taquería

SERVES 6 • PREP TIME: 15 MINUTES • COOK TIME: 12 HOURS (LOW)

❦ *Shredded beef tacos are some of the most delicious foods you will ever eat if you are lucky enough to live near an authentic taqueria or find one in your travels. This recipe looks complicated, but it results in drippy, spicy, slightly tangy, slightly sweet tacos that you'll find yourself making again and again. Prepare these tacos with soft flour tortillas— either white or whole wheat is fine. Warm the tortillas for just a few minutes, and then add the meat, some onions, cheese, and fresh cilantro instead of lettuce. This recipe makes enough for you to have leftovers. Freeze the leftover meat for up to 3 months, and you can have these whenever you crave them.*

4 dried pasilla chiles

1 dried guajillo chile

1 dried mulato chile

1 medium onion, chopped

3 garlic cloves

¼ cup fresh lime juice

3 chipotles in adobo

2 tablespoons tomato paste

1 tablespoon honey

2 teaspoons ground cumin

1 teaspoon smoked paprika

1 teaspoon dried Mexican oregano

Cooking spray

½ cup chopped fresh cilantro

3 pounds lean, boneless beef roast

12 flour tortillas

Grated cheese, salsa, and other favorite toppings

The Night Before

1. In a comal or a heavy frying pan over medium-high heat, add the dried chiles and quickly toast them on all sides, no longer than 2 minutes total.

2. Remove the chiles to a bowl and cover them with hot water. Let them soak overnight at room temperature.

Continued

In the Morning

1. In a blender, pour the chiles and their soaking water into a blender along with the onion, garlic, lime juice, chipotles, tomato paste, honey, cumin, smoked paprika, and oregano. Blend until smooth. Taste and adjust the seasonings as desired.

2. Spray the slow cooker with cooking spray.

3. Into the slow cooker, pour half of the sauce and add the meat and then the rest of the sauce so the meat is fully submerged. Cook on low for 11½ hours.

4. Add the cilantro and cook for another 30 minutes.

5. Transfer the beef to a cutting board and shred it using two forks, and then transfer the meat to a serving bowl and stir in a little of the sauce from the slow cooker to moisten it.

6. Warm the tortillas in a dry skillet over medium-high heat.

7. Spoon the meat into the warm tortillas and top with your favorite toppings.

Cooking Tip: Don't throw out the liquid left in the slow cooker when your meat is cooked. Use this highly flavored liquid as a base for soups or as a sauce to add to other dishes. Taste it and check for seasoning before using. Keep leftover sauce in the refrigerator for up to a week or freeze it for longer storage.

BEEF STEW WITH CHOPPED VEGGIES

Ropa Vieja

SERVES 6 • PREP TIME: 15 MINUTES • COOK TIME: 10 HOURS (LOW), 5 HOURS (HIGH)

ŶŶŶ *In Spanish this recipe is called* ropa vieja, *literally "old clothes," referring to the shredded beef and vegetable pieces in this tender, flavorful stew. This is a Cuban recipe very popular in other Caribbean countries. Since the vegetables are chopped into small pieces, they nearly disintegrate into the stock, leaving only flavor and nutrition behind. If your family doesn't like spicy foods, leave the habanero out or replace it with a less spicy chile such as poblano.*

Cooking spray

3 pounds lean, boneless beef roast

4 cups Beef Stock (see page 47)

4 celery ribs, chopped

3 poblano chiles, diced

2 red bell peppers, diced

2 carrots, chopped

1 onion, chopped

1 habanero chile, left whole

1 bay leaf

4 garlic cloves, crushed

2 large tomatoes, diced

1 teaspoon dried Mexican oregano

1 teaspoon ground cumin

1 teaspoon sea salt

½ cup sliced Spanish olives

1. Spray the slow cooker with cooking spray.

2. In the slow cooker, combine all the ingredients, except the olives, and cook on low for 10 hours or on high for 5 hours.

3. Remove the habanero.

4. Transfer the beef to a cutting board and shred it using two forks. Return the shredded beef to the slow cooker and stir it into the broth.

5. Serve with rice topped with the olives.

BRAISED BEEF AND PORK WITH GREEN SALSA

Guisado de Cerdo y Res con Salsa Verde

SERVES 6 · PREP TIME: 5 MINUTES · COOK TIME: 18 HOURS (LOW)

Although this is an easy dish to make, it does take a very long time to cook. You cook the seasoned meat first, drain out any accumulated fat, shred it, and then cook it again with Green Salsa until it is indescribably delicious. The cooking time is very long, but it needs no supervision and very little preparation. It's best to begin this after dinner the night before you wish to serve it. The meat almost disintegrates in your mouth—it's that tender. You can use it in any dish that calls for cooked meat, from tacos to tortas.

Cooking spray

1½ pounds lean, boneless beef roast

1½ pounds lean, boneless pork roast

2 tablespoons Fajita Seasoning Mix (see page 157)

1 cup Green Salsa (see page 153) or 1 (14.5-ounce) can green enchilada sauce

2 poblano chiles, fire-roasted, peeled, seeded, and diced (see page 158)

The Night Before

1. Spray the slow cooker with cooking spray.

2. Rub the fajita seasoning all over the beef and pork.

3. In the slow cooker, place the meat, and cook on low for 10 hours

In the Morning

1. Transfer the meat to a cutting board and drain the liquid from the slow cooker (save it for sauces and stocks). Shred the meat using two forks.

2. In the slow cooker, place the shredded meat, cover it with the Green Salsa and poblanos, and cook for 8 hours on low.

3. Use the meat in tostadas, enchiladas, tacos, burritos, or tortas.

Cooking Tip: This dish freezes very well for up to 6 months. You can save a lot of time if you make a big batch, let it cool, and then freeze it in recipe-size portions. Figure about ½ cup per person for most dishes.

SMOKY BEER-BRAISED PORK TACOS

Cerdo a la Cerveza para Tacos

SERVES 6 ● PREP TIME: 5 MINUTES ●
COOK TIME: 8 TO 10 HOURS (LOW), 4½ TO 5½ HOURS (HIGH)

🍴 *Soft flour tortillas are filled with seasoned tender pork. It doesn't get much simpler than that, and when the ingredients are this flavorful, you don't need much more than a squeeze of fresh lime and a sprinkle of cheese. Flour tortillas are called for in this recipe, but you can certainly substitute corn tortillas, crisp taco shells, or even tostadas. Add the toppings your family likes best—cheese, onions, salsa, avocados, and the rest. Serve with Classic Refried Beans (see page 125) for a hearty, stick-to-your ribs meal.*

Cooking spray

2 pounds lean, boneless pork roast

1 teaspoon cumin

½ teaspoon sea salt

½ teaspoon freshly ground black pepper

3 garlic cloves, minced

1 tablespoon liquid smoke

1 medium onion, chopped

1½ cups chopped fresh cilantro

1 cup Red Salsa (see page 41)
or Green Salsa (see page 153)

½ cup Chicken Stock (see page 46)

½ cup beer

3 medium jalapeños, seeded and chopped

12 (8-inch) flour tortillas, warmed

1. Spray the slow cooker with cooking spray

2. Rub the meat with the cumin, salt, and pepper.

3. In the slow cooker, combine all the ingredients except the tortillas, and cook on low for 8 to 10 hours or on high for 4½ to 5½ hours, until the meat is tender.

4. Warm the tortillas in a dry skillet over medium-high heat.

5. Shred the meat using two forks, spoon a generous amount onto each tortilla, and serve with your favorite toppings.

SMOKY PORK STEW WITH HOMINY AND GREEN SALSA

Guisado de Cerdo y Maíz para Pozole en Salsa Verde

SERVES 6 • PREP TIME: 15 MINUTES • COOK TIME: 10 HOURS (LOW), 5½ HOURS (HIGH)

This stew, also called guisado verde, *is made with tomatillos. It is simplified here, using green salsa, either jarred or homemade (see page 153). Both smoked salt and smoked paprika are used to add a "just taken off the grill" flavor to the stew. Sear the meat in a hot frying pan before you put it in the slow cooker. This gives it added flavor and a better texture. If you want to do this step ahead of time, you can. Just refrigerate the meat overnight after searing. If you can't find hominy or if your family doesn't like it, add corn instead. It's not quite the same, but it works.*

1 teaspoon smoked salt

½ teaspoon freshly ground black pepper

½ teaspoon smoked paprika

3 pounds lean, boneless pork roast

2 tablespoons olive oil

1 large onion, chopped

2 cups Green Salsa (see page 153)

6 garlic cloves

4 to 6 jalapeños, seeded and sliced

4 bottles Mexican beer, such as Corona, Sol, or Negra Modelo

¾ cup chopped fresh cilantro

1½ teaspoons dried Mexican oregano

2 (15.5-ounce) cans white hominy, rinsed and drained

The Night Before

1. In a small bowl, combine the salt, pepper, and smoked paprika. Rub this spice mixture over the meat to cover it completely.

2. In a heavy frying pan over medium-high heat, heat the olive oil. When the oil is hot and just beginning to smoke, add the meat to the pan and sear it on all sides. Transfer the meat to a storage container, but leave it uncovered.

3. Add the onions to the pan; sauté for 1 minute until they begin to soften. Remove the cooked onions to the storage container with the beef. When the ingredients have cooled, seal the container and place it in the refrigerator.

In the Morning

1. In the slow cooker, combine the meat and onions, the garlic, the jalapeños, and the beer, and cook on low for 10 hours or on high for 5½ hours.

2. Stir in the cilantro, oregano, and hominy, and cook for another 15 minutes just to heat the hominy.

3. Serve with a little diced avocado and grated cheese on top, if desired.

PORK WITH RED CHILE SAUCE

Cerdo en Salsa Roja

SERVES 6 · PREP TIME: 5 MINUTES · COOK TIME: 8 HOURS (LOW)

❦ *The most difficult part of this spectacular dish is cutting the pork into chunks, and you don't have to do that if you don't want to. Just shred the meat at the end of cooking time instead. The shredded meat isn't quite as pretty on the plate as the chunks, but looks aren't everything. Serve this with rice or Corn on the Cob with Chili and Lime (see page 122), a big bowl of tortilla chips, and salad on the side.*

2 tablespoons Taco Seasoning Mix (see page 156)

3 pounds lean, boneless pork roast, cut into bite-size chunks

2 medium onions, cut into chunks

3 garlic cloves, chopped

1¼ cups Chicken Stock (see page 46)

2 tablespoons chili powder

1 teaspoon smoked paprika

1 teaspoon ground cumin

1 teaspoon dried Mexican oregano

1 teaspoon packed brown sugar

¼ cup tomato paste

½ cup Mexican crema or sour cream

1. Rub the taco seasoning all over the pork.

2. In the slow cooker, combine the pork, onions, and garlic.

3. In a medium bowl, whisk together the chicken stock, chili powder, paprika, cumin, oregano, brown sugar, and tomato paste. Pour this mixture over the meat in the slow cooker, and cook on low for 8 hours.

4. Stir in the crema, and cook for 5 minutes more, uncovered, before serving.

Ingredient Tip: The pork makes a fantastic taco or enchilada filling. Shred the meat at the end of cooking time and serve it in tortillas with your favorite toppings.

RED CHILE AND PORK STEW

Carne Adovada Estilo Nuevo México

SERVES 6 ● PREP TIME: 15 MINUTES ● COOK TIME: 8 HOURS (LOW), 5 HOURS (HIGH)

Yes, the amount of red chile powder is correct—and no, this dish won't blow the top of your head off. New Mexico red chile powder is mild, even in large amounts, and this stew is not at all spicy. It has a warm, comforting heat that will keep you going back for more. Serve it with corn tortillas and your favorite side dish. If you have leftovers, fry some eggs for breakfast and serve them with this stew.

1 cup New Mexico red chile powder

6 cups Chicken Stock (see page 46), divided

3 pounds lean, boneless pork roast

3 medium onions, cut into chunks

6 garlic cloves, chopped

2 teaspoons dried Mexican oregano

1. In a blender, process the chile powder and 3 cups of the chicken stock until smooth.

2. In the slow cooker, whisk this mixture with the rest of the stock until the mixture is well blended. Add the rest of the ingredients.

3. Cook on low for 8 hours or on high for 5 hours, until the pork is very tender.

4. Shred or chop the pork and serve it with Classic Refried Beans (see page 125), rice, and warm flour tortillas.

Ingredient Tip: Be sure you get New Mexican red chile powder. If you try to make this with any other type of chile powder, you may spontaneously combust. If you can't find it in a store, there are plenty of sources on the Internet.

YUCATEC-STYLE SLOW-ROASTED PORK

Cochinita Pibil

SERVES 6 • PREP TIME: 10 MINUTES • COOK TIME: 8 TO 10 HOURS ON LOW

Marinating and then slow cooking the pork in this sweet, tangy, spicy marinade infuses the meat with an unbelievable amount of flavor and keeps it tender, too. Authentic cochinita pibil *is made with juice from the sour orange, but since it isn't readily available in many areas of the United States, you can substitute a combination of sweet orange juice and tangy lime juice. Achiote paste is another ingredient that can be hard to find locally—if you can't find it in the imported foods section of your grocery store, skip it. Though traditional to the dish, there are plenty of spices here besides achiote paste to flavor the pork.*

FOR THE PORK ROAST

2 pounds pork butt roast with bone

2 tablespoons achiote paste

½ cup orange juice

¼ cup lime juice

1 tablespoon Mexican oregano

1 teaspoon ground cumin

1 teaspoon smoked paprika

1 teaspoon chili powder

1 teaspoon ground coriander

1 teaspoon chopped garlic

½ teaspoon ground cinnamon

½ teaspoon ground allspice

Pinch salt

Pinch freshly ground black pepper

12 corn tortillas

FOR THE RELISH

½ cup grated or finely chopped radishes

¼ cup minced red onion

1 seeded and minced habanero chile pepper

¼ cup orange juice

2 tablespoons lime juice

2 tablespoons water

¼ teaspoon kosher salt

¼ cup chopped cilantro

The Night Before

1. Poke holes all over the pork with a fork. Rub the achiote paste all over the meat. Set aside.

2. In a large bowl, mix together the orange juice and lime juice. Then add in the cumin, paprika, chili powder, coriander, garlic, cinnamon, allspice, salt, and pepper.

3. Submerge the pork in the mixture, cover, and refrigerate overnight.

In the Morning

1. To the slow cooker, add the pork and its overnight marinade.

2. Cook on low for 8 to 10 hours. The longer it cooks, the more tender it will be.

3. During the last hour of cooking, in a medium bowl mix together all of the ingredients for the relish. Let stand for at least 10 minute to allow the flavors to blend.

4. When the cooking is over, open the lid and shred the pork with two forks.

5. To serve, spoon the contents of the slow cooker into tortillas, and top with the relish.

SWEET AND SAVORY PORK RIBS WITH GREEN MOLE

Costillas de Cerdo en Mole Verde

SERVES 6 · PREP TIME: 15 MINUTES · COOK TIME: 4 HOURS (LOW), 2 HOURS (HIGH)

❦❦ *One of the best ways to cook ribs is to start them in a slow cooker, and then crisp them up on the grill or under the broiler. Slow cooking brings out all the flavor and tenderness while keeping them moist, and a few minutes under the broiler gives them that great caramelized flavor. Here, the ribs are slow cooked in a green mole sauce that makes them even more tender and flavorful. If you want to finish them on the grill instead of under the broiler, go right ahead. It will work just fine. Serve the ribs with ripe summer tomatoes, sliced thickly and sprinkled with salt and pepper.*

1½ pounds tomatillos with husks removed or 1 (28-ounce) can tomatillos, cut into bite-size pieces

¼ cup diced fire-roasted poblano chiles (see page 158)

1 medium onion, chopped

2 serrano chiles, seeded and chopped

2 teaspoons honey

4 garlic cloves, minced

1 teaspoon ground coriander

½ teaspoon ground cumin

½ teaspoon sea salt

1 tablespoon Fajita Seasoning Mix (see page 157)

2½ to 3 pounds pork loin back ribs

½ cup chopped fresh cilantro

2 tablespoons fresh lime juice

1. In a blender, combine the tomatillos, poblanos, onion, serranos, honey, garlic, coriander, cumin, and salt. Pulse until smooth.

2. Rub the fajita seasoning all over the ribs.

3. In the slow cooker, combine the ribs and tomatillo mixture, and cook on low for 4 hours or on high for 2 hours.

4. Remove the ribs from the slow cooker and broil them under the highest heat until they begin to brown, about 10 minutes. Watch them carefully.

5. Skim any fat from the sauce in the slow cooker. In a medium saucepan over medium heat, simmer the sauce from the slow cooker for 10 minutes to thicken it. Stir the cilantro and lime juice into the sauce and serve it with the ribs.

SPICED PORK ROAST

Asado de Cerdo a las Especias

SERVES 6 ◦ PREP TIME: 5 MINUTES, PLUS MARINATING TIME ◦
COOK TIME: 8 HOURS (LOW), 4 HOURS (HIGH)

❦ *Pork roast doesn't have to be a complex meal. This is easy to make in a slow cooker, and the sweet, spicy rub has a chance to flavor the meat all the way through. The aroma of cocoa and chipotle will fill the house with a mouthwatering aroma that will get bellies rumbling. The chipotle is enough to give your lips a tingle, but if you like more heat, then add a little more chipotle. If you happen to have a slow cooker with a meat thermometer attachment, stop cooking when it reaches 145°F.*

2 tablespoons packed brown sugar

1½ tablespoons chipotle powder

2 teaspoons sea salt

2 teaspoons chili powder

1½ teaspoons unsweetened cocoa powder

1 teaspoon ground cumin

1 teaspoon smoked paprika

1 teaspoon dried Mexican oregano

1 teaspoon garlic powder

½ teaspoon ground roasted cinnamon

½ teaspoon freshly ground black pepper

2 pounds sirloin tip pork roast or similar quality pork roast

2 tablespoons olive oil

½ cup Vegetable Stock (see page 48)

The Night Before

1. In a medium bowl, combine all the ingredients except the pork roast, olive oil, and vegetable stock.

2. Rub the spice mixture and the olive oil all over the roast, coating it completely on all sides.

3. Cover the roast tightly with plastic wrap and refrigerate it overnight.

In the Morning

1. Pour the vegetable stock into the slow cooker, add the roast, and cook on low for 8 hours or on high for 4 hours, until the roast is fork tender.

2. Turn off the heat and let the roast stand for 10 minutes before serving.

8

SIDE DISHES

~~~~~~~~~~

While Mexican food has many different accompaniments like salsa, cheese, and guacamole, the side dishes are usually quite understated. Beans, corn, and rice are a large part of Mexican cooking, but local favorites like *calabacitas* (summer squash) and potatoes also play a part. Sometimes the very best way to go is with a simple salad or sliced ripe summer tomatoes still warm from the sun.

When you need something heartier, you'll find great ideas here. Pinto beans are generally the beans of choice in these recipes. They cook down easily, have a mild flavor, and are inexpensive. They are an excellent bean for the slow cooker because they cook relatively quickly. Rice can also be cooked in a slow cooker, but it doesn't take very long, so you'll need to make it on a day when you are going to be home. Another option is an electric rice cooker, which turns off automatically when the rice is cooked.

Most vegetables are too tender to handle a long time in the slow cooker and will turn to mush. Only use recipes specifically created for slow cooking.

CORN ON THE COB WITH CHILI AND LIME

Elotes con Limón y Chile

SERVES 6 · PREP TIME: 5 MINUTES · COOK TIME: 4½ HOURS (LOW), 2 HOURS (HIGH)

Fresh corn on the cob is a delicious part of summer meals. This recipe goes beyond the plain corn on the cob and takes it to the level of Mexican street food with the addition of chili powder and lime. If you've never cooked corn in the slow cooker before, you are in for a treat. Since the corn steams inside the aluminum foil instead of boiling in water, it doesn't lose any of its flavor. When you unwrap the packets, you'll have perfectly cooked, tender, buttery corn with the refreshing flavor of chili and lime. Best of all, this method is great when you are cooking for a crowd. Just be aware that a full slow cooker may take a bit more time.

6 tablespoons unsalted butter, at room temperature

1½ tablespoons fresh lime juice

1½ teaspoons chili powder

½ teaspoon ancho chili powder

1 teaspoon sea salt

½ teaspoon freshly ground black pepper

1 tablespoon lime zest

6 ears corn on the cob, husks and silk removed

1. In a medium bowl, mix together the butter, lime juice, chili powders, salt, pepper, and lime zest until well blended.

2. Cut six large squares of aluminum foil, and place an ear of corn in the center of each square. Cover each ear of corn with 1 tablespoon of the butter mixture.

3. In the slow cooker, place the corn wrapped tightly in the foil, and cook on low for 4½ hours or on high for 2 hours.

4. Unwrap the corn and add more seasonings if needed. Serve hot.

Warning: Be careful when you open the packets of hot corn. Steam will come out as soon as you tear it open. Don't put your face near the packet, and never let children open the packets by themselves.

CILANTRO AND LIME RICE

Arroz Verde

SERVES 6 • PREP TIME: 5 MINUTES • COOK TIME: 4 HOURS (LOW), 2 HOURS (HIGH)

This rice cooks until it is moist and fluffy, then lime zest, lime juice, and a generous amount of cilantro are stirred in. The lime and cilantro give the rice a fresh flavor that goes especially well with fish and poultry dishes. The rice can be refrigerated for up to one week. You could make a big batch of it and refrigerate it for use in burritos, tacos, and numerous other dishes all week long. These are the recipes that make your life so much easier.

3 cups water

2 tablespoons unsalted butter

1 teaspoon sea salt

1½ cups uncooked long-grain white rice

2 teaspoons lime zest

3 teaspoons fresh lime juice

1 cup chopped fresh cilantro, divided

1. In the slow cooker, mix the water, butter, salt, and rice , and cook on low for 4 hours or on high for 2 hours.

2. Stir in the lime zest, juice, and ¾ cup of cilantro.

3. Top with the remaining ¼ cup of cilantro and serve.

STEWED SUMMER SQUASH

Calabacitas Guisadas

SERVES 6 · PREP TIME: 5 MINUTES · COOK TIME: 5 HOURS (LOW), 2½ HOURS (HIGH)

If you've never liked zucchini before, try it in this dish. As the squash cooks, it gets more and more tender and absorbs the garlicky, slightly spicy sauce. You know how some zucchini recipes stop when the vegetables are al dente? Well, not this recipe. Serve this over cornbread for a light lunch, or add a small bowl of it alongside your main course. If you like your food on the spicy side, substitute habanero Jack cheese for the pepper Jack.

6 zucchini, cut into ½-inch-thick slices

2 teaspoons olive oil

1 medium onion, thinly sliced

2 garlic cloves, minced

1 (14.5-ounce) can diced tomatoes
   with chiles

1 cup grated pepper Jack cheese

1. In the slow cooker, combine all the ingredients except the cheese, and cook on low for 5 hours or on high for 2½ hours, until the zucchini is tender.

2. Add the cheese to the top and let stand for 5 minutes before serving.

   Ingredient Variation: This makes a really good main course if you add 1½ pounds of cooked lean ground beef to the zucchini and tomatoes. The result is somewhere between a soup and a stew and is especially good with tortilla chips.

CLASSIC REFRIED BEANS

Frijoles Refritos

SERVES 6 • PREP TIME: 10 MINUTES • COOK TIME: 8 HOURS (LOW), 4½ HOURS (HIGH)

Refried beans are a staple side dish and an accompaniment of many main dishes in Mexican cuisine. They aren't hard to make at all, plus they freeze well for up to 3 months, so you can make a big batch and freeze them in recipe-size portions for use later on. Always add salt at the very end when cooking beans, because salt keeps them from getting tender. Use these refried beans as a side dish or in burritos, nachos, or enchiladas.

1¼ cups dried pinto beans, rinsed

1 medium onion, chopped

1 jalapeño, seeded and chopped

2 garlic cloves, minced

4 cups water or Vegetable Stock
  (see page 48)

2 teaspoons sea salt

1 teaspoon freshly ground black pepper

½ teaspoon ancho chili powder

¼ teaspoon ground cumin

1. In the slow cooker, combine the beans, onion, jalapeño, garlic, and water, and stir to blend. Cook on low for 8 hours or on high for 4½ hours, until the beans are tender.

2. Drain any remaining liquid off the beans and reserve it.

3. Add the salt, black pepper, chili powder, and cumin to the beans, and stir well to combine.

4. Mash the beans with a potato masher, adding bean liquid as needed to get the correct consistency. Serve warm.

SMOKY RESTAURANT-STYLE BEANS

Frijoles Estilo Restaurante

SERVES 6 • PREP TIME: 15 MINUTES • COOK TIME: 8 HOURS (LOW)

This is a smoky, spicy bean side dish that is very versatile. You can eat the beans as they are, spoon them over rice or cornbread, or use them to perk up soups and stews. The smoky flavor complements everything from barbacoa to Texas barbecue, and since they freeze well, you can make a big batch and freeze leftovers for another time. Taste these just before serving and decide if they need salt or not—it's very easy to oversalt beans, so be conservative.

½ pound bacon, diced

¼ pound Mexican chorizo, removed from its casing

4 cups Beef Stock (see page 47), boiling hot

1¼ cups dried pinto beans, rinsed

1 medium onion, chopped

1 large tomato, diced

1½ jalapeños, seeded and sliced

2 tablespoons chopped chipotles in adobo

4 garlic cloves, chopped

1 tablespoon liquid smoke

1 teaspoon smoked paprika

1 teaspoon ground cumin

The Night Before

In a medium skillet over medium-high heat, fry the bacon and chorizo until cooked through, about 5 minutes. When the food cools, place in a storage container and refrigerate overnight.

In the Morning

1. In the slow cooker, combine the bacon and chorizo with the beef stock, beans, onion, tomato, jalapeños, chipotles, and garlic, and cook on low for 8 hours.

2. Add the liquid smoke, smoked paprika, and cumin.

3. Stir the beans, taste and adjust seasonings as necessary, and serve hot.

DRUNKEN BEANS

Frijoles Borrachos

SERVES 6 • PREP TIME: 15 MINUTES • COOK TIME: 1 HOUR (HIGH) PLUS 7 HOURS (LOW)

❦ *These beans are not usually served mashed or refried. They are generally added to your plate as is with the main dish and rice. For the best flavor, use Mexican beer or another light beer in this recipe. Dark beer will be overpowering and will make your house smell like an Old West saloon—and not in a good way. These beans do freeze well, so make a big batch once a month. It's best to make this recipe on the weekend. As you'll see, the slow cooker requires more monitoring than the standard recipe due to the three different stages of use. Taste the beans before you decide they're not worth it.*

4 cups water

1¼ cups dried pinto beans, rinsed

½ pound bacon, diced

1 medium onion, chopped

1 large tomato, diced

2 jalapeños, seeded and sliced

4 garlic cloves, chopped

12 ounces Mexican light beer

½ teaspoon sea salt

1 teaspoon smoked paprika

¼ cup chopped fresh cilantro

1. In the slow cooker, combine the water and beans, and cook on high for 1 hour.

2. Meanwhile, in a medium skillet over medium-high heat, fry the bacon until it is evenly browned but still tender, about 4 minutes. Drain off half the fat from the bacon.

3. Add the onion to the skillet, and cook for 2 minutes, or until the onion is soft.

4. After the beans have cooked in the slow cooker for 1 hour, add the onion, bacon, tomato, jalapeños, and garlic to the slow cooker.

5. Cook on low for 6 hours. Lift the cover and add the beer, salt, smoked paprika, and cilantro.

6. Cook on low for 1 hour more, then serve hot.

Ingredient Tip: If your beans don't get tender within 8 hours, they are probably old. Always check the sell-by date, and if the beans have been around for a while, soak them in water overnight before cooking.

9

DESSERTS

~~~~~~~~~~~~~~~~~~~~~~~~~~~~

Having a little something sweet to end a meal gives you closure, especially if you have a sweet tooth. For many people dessert is the entire reason for getting through the vegetable course.

When you can whip up an easy dessert in your slow cooker, there isn't any reason to end a meal without that sugary goodness. In Mexico, after the main meal of the day, custard or pudding might be served, followed by coffee and fresh fruit. Cakes, cookies, and sweet rolls are sometimes eaten for breakfast, and there are plenty of excuses throughout the day to eat a sweet snack.

If you don't have time to make a dessert, fresh fruit always works. Pineapple, oranges, melons, mangoes, papayas, and bananas are just a few of the fruits that could signify the end of a meal. In Mexico, a lot of people enjoy red chili powder on fresh fruit, though not necessarily for dessert. The recipes you'll find in this chapter aren't really for authentic Mexican desserts, but the flavors and textures capture the spirit of Mexican cuisine.

CARAMEL RICE PUDDING

Arroz con Leche y Cajeta

SERVES 6 · PREP TIME: 5 MINUTES · COOK TIME: 2 HOURS (LOW)

Even if you've never liked rice pudding, you should take a stab at this version. It is creamy and sweet, with an intense vanilla flavor that comes from both vanilla extract and vanilla bean. You'd think that this would be one of those desserts that makes your teeth hurt from the sweetness, but the combination of bland rice and the use of cajeta helps keep the flavors in balance.

Cooking spray

2 cinnamon sticks

2 teaspoons pure vanilla extract

1 vanilla bean, halved lengthwise

1 (14-ounce) can sweetened
    condensed milk

1 cup canned cajeta

1½ cups whole milk

½ cup raisins

3 cups cooked white rice

1. Spray the slow cooker with cooking spray.

2. In the slow cooker, combine all the ingredients except the rice, stirring gently until well blended.

3. Stir in the rice, and cook on low for 2 hours, or until the pudding is thick and creamy.

4. Remove the vanilla pod and cinnamon sticks, and serve warm.

Ingredient Tip: Cajeta is similar to dulce de leche and caramel sauce, but it is not quite the same. Cajeta is made from goat's milk, which gives it a more complex flavor than the other two. It is luxuriously creamy, with a spicy, tangy flavor and a balanced sweetness that is not at all cloying. Look for it in the Mexican foods or baking section of your grocery store. If you can't find it, you can substitute dulce de leche, but the flavor will not be the same.

CARAMEL FLAN

Flan de Caramelo

SERVES 6 • PREP TIME: 10 MINUTES • COOK TIME: 4 HOURS (HIGH)

Flan is a smooth custard that is one of the best-known desserts of Mexico. It is tricky to make the conventional way—all too often the custard curdles and is not silky smooth as it's supposed to be. When you make it in a slow cooker, the heat stays constant, and there is less chance of it curdling and separating. For your first attempt at this recipe, plan on staying home for the entire cooking time. Depending on how your slow cooker heats, it could take less or more time to set.

3 tablespoons unsalted butter

¾ cup sugar

5 eggs

1 (12-ounce) can evaporated milk

1 (14-ounce) can dulce de leche

4 ounces cream cheese, cut into
  1-inch cubes

1 teaspoon pure vanilla extract

Vanilla sea salt (optional)

1. Grease 6 (4-ounce) ramekins with the butter.

2. In a blender, add the sugar, eggs, evaporated milk, dulce de leche, cream cheese, and vanilla, and blend until smooth.

3. On the bottom of the slow cooker, place a folded tea towel.

4. Pour the flan mixture into the ramekins and arrange the ramekins on the towel in the slow cooker. Cover the ramekins tightly with foil.

5. Pour warm water into the slow cooker until it reaches halfway up the sides of the ramekins. (Make sure the water reaches no more than halfway up the sides—it will ruin the flans if it splashes into the ramekins.)

6. Cook on high for 4 hours. Then remove the ramekins from the slow cooker, take off the aluminum foil, and let them cool for at least an hour in the refrigerator.

7. Sprinkle with the vanilla sea salt (if using) just before serving.

Cooking Tip: Small, 4-ounce wide-mouth jelly jars make excellent ramekins, and the screw-on tops work perfectly to keep out excess moisture while the flans cook. They can be found in the baking section of grocery and variety stores and aren't very expensive at all.

DULCE DE LECHE FONDUE

Fondue de Dulce de Leche

SERVES 6 · PREP TIME: 5 MINUTES · COOK TIME: 2 HOURS (LOW), 1 HOUR (HIGH)

Dulce de leche *is caramelized sweetened milk. It is richer and has a more complex flavor than caramel. You can usually find it in the Mexican foods or baking section of your grocery store. If it isn't available in your area, you can easily find it on the Internet. Fondue is a fun, casual dessert. You can use almost anything for dippers—choose the things you like best. You'll need a small 1- or 1½-quart slow cooker for this recipe. Pass a small container of flaked salt at the table for those guests who like salted caramel.*

1 (14-ounce) can dulce de leche

1 tablespoon rum

Dipping options: pound cake squares, brownie squares, apple slices, pineapple chunks, marshmallows, pretzels, chocolate, or whatever you like

1. In the slow cooker, cook the dulce de leche on low for 2 hours or on high for 1 hour, or until it is melted and smooth.

2. Stir in the rum.

3. Keep the slow cooker on its warm setting and serve the fondue with the various dippers.

LIME POTS DE CRÈME

Pots de Crème de Limón

SERVES 6 • PREP TIME: 5 MINUTES
COOK TIME: 2 HOURS (HIGH), PLUS 3 HOURS COOLING TIME

Key lime pie is a delicious finish to almost any Mexican meal, but when you don't have the time to make a pie from scratch, give these Lime Pots de Crème a try. The flavor is very much like Key lime pie, but there is a little kick of tequila that is unmistakable. If you can't find Key lime juice at your grocery store, substitute regular fresh lime juice. The slow cooker creates a texture that is so silky and creamy that everyone will wonder how you did it.

3 tablespoons unsalted butter

4 egg yolks

1 (14-ounce) can sweetened condensed milk

½ cup Key lime juice

2 teaspoons lime zest, plus more for serving

1 tablespoon tequila

Whipped cream, for serving

1. Grease 6 (4-ounce) ramekins or pots de crème cups with the butter.

2. In a medium bowl, whisk the egg yolks and the condensed milk until well blended. Add the lime juice, lime zest, and tequila, and stir until smooth and well blended.

3. Place a folded tea towel on the bottom of the slow cooker.

4. Pour the lime mixture into the ramekins and arrange the ramekins on the towel in the slow cooker.

5. Pour warm water into the slow cooker until it reaches halfway up the sides of the ramekins. (Make sure the water reaches no more than halfway up the sides—it will ruin the pots de crème if it splashes into the ramekins.) Lay a clean kitchen towel over the top of the slow cooker, and secure the lid on top of the towel.

6. Cook on high for 2 hours.

7. Remove the lime pots de crème from the slow cooker. Let them cool to room temperature, and then refrigerate them for 3 hours.

8. Top with a dollop of whipped cream and a sprinkling of lime zest before serving.

DARK CHOCOLATE BROWNIES

Brownies de Chocolate Amargo

MAKES 14 TO 16 BROWNIES · PREP TIME: 10 MINUTES ·
COOK TIME: 4 HOURS (LOW), PLUS 3 HOURS COOLING TIME

Dark, rich, gooey chocolate brownies with the warmth of roasted cinnamon and chipotle are the perfect way to end any meal or to satisfy that midafternoon craving. The chipotle gives a little tingle to your lips with every bite, but it isn't actually hot. You can adjust the amount to your personal tastes or leave it out completely. When the cooking time is up, the brownies will still look pretty raw. Don't worry, they will continue to cook in the retained heat of the slow cooker liner. Let them cool for at least 3 hours before serving, no matter how tempted you are to eat one.

Cooking spray

1¼ cups all-purpose flour

¼ cup unsweetened extra-dark cocoa powder

¾ teaspoon baking powder

½ teaspoon ground roasted cinnamon

½ teaspoon sea salt

½ teaspoon chipotle powder

8 ounces Mexican or bittersweet chocolate, chopped

½ cup unsalted butter, cut into small pieces

1 cup sugar

3 eggs, beaten

1 cup dark chocolate chips

1. Spray the slow cooker with cooking spray, line the bottom with parchment paper, and then spray the parchment paper with cooking spray.

2. In a medium bowl, whisk together the flour, cocoa powder, baking powder, cinnamon, salt, and chipotle powder. Set aside.

3. In a large microwave-safe bowl, microwave the bittersweet chocolate and butter until the mixture is melted, stirring every 30 seconds.

4. Stir the sugar into the melted chocolate mixture, and then beat in the eggs.

5. Add the dry ingredients and chocolate chips to the wet ingredients and fold them in just until moistened. Don't overmix.

6. Spoon the batter into the slow cooker and smooth the top with the back of a large spoon.

7. Cook on low for 3½ hours; then remove the slow cooker lid, and cook for another 30 minutes.

8. Remove the crock insert from the cooker. Run a knife around the edge of the brownies to loosen them from the insert. Let them cool completely in the crock, about 3 hours.

9. The brownies won't look done, but they will be perfect after 3 hours of cooling.

Ingredient Tip: Cacao, from which chocolate is made, was beloved by the Maya and the Aztec (chocolate as we know it was invented in Europe). It was so valued that cacao beans were sometimes traded and used like money. They were sometimes counterfeited by filling the empty shells with mud.

CHOCOLATE MOCHA COBBLER

Pastel de Chocolate y Mocha

SERVES 6 TO 8 · PREP TIME: 15 MINUTES · COOK TIME: 4 HOURS (LOW)

❦ *Serve the cobbler warm and add a generous scoop of vanilla or salted caramel ice cream to each serving. The cold ice cream will begin to melt into the hot cake and dark chocolate sauce, and the result is a truly magical combination of textures and temperatures.*

FOR THE SAUCE

1¼ cups packed brown sugar

⅓ cup unsweetened extra-dark cocoa powder

Pinch freshly grated nutmeg

½ teaspoon ancho chili powder

1 teaspoon ground roasted cinnamon

2½ cups hot dark-roast coffee

4 tablespoons unsalted butter, cut into small pieces

FOR THE CAKE

1 cup all-purpose flour

¾ cup granulated sugar

¼ cup unsweetened extra-dark cocoa powder

½ teaspoon baking powder

½ teaspoon sea salt

1 cup whole milk

1 teaspoon pure vanilla extract

1 cup bittersweet chocolate chips

Cooking spray

To make the sauce

1. In a large microwave-safe bowl, mix together the brown sugar, cocoa powder, nutmeg, ancho chili powder, and cinnamon.

2. Whisk in the coffee, and add the butter to the bowl. Microwave on high for 5 minutes, or until it is bubbling. Whisk to blend the sauce, and set aside.

To make the cake batter

1. In a large bowl, whisk together the flour, granulated sugar, cocoa powder, baking powder, and salt.

2. Stir in the milk and vanilla, and fold in the chocolate chips.

To make the cobbler

1. Spray the slow cooker with cooking spray.

2. In the slow cooker, add the cake batter, and pour the hot chocolate sauce over the top of the batter but do not stir. Cook on low for 4 hours.

3. Remove the lid, turn off the heat, and allow the cobbler to stand for 10 minutes before serving. The sauce will thicken as it stands.

CHOCOLATE RICE PUDDING

Arroz con Leche y Chocolate

SERVES 6 • PREP TIME: 5 MINUTES • COOK TIME: 8 HOURS (LOW), 4 HOURS (HIGH)

Chocolate Rice Pudding is not for people who are lukewarm about sweets. Rich and creamy, this rice pudding is loaded with chocolate and a touch of coffee, too. Because it cooks so slowly, the rice has a chance to absorb all the flavor it can hold, and the texture becomes lush and velvety. It's the perfect ending to warming soups or stews on cold winter nights, and it is also fantastic after an alfresco meal of grilled meat and salad in the summertime.

Cooking spray

1 cup uncooked Arborio rice

3 cups half-and-half

1 (14-ounce) can sweetened
  condensed milk

¼ cup coffee liqueur

8 ounces Mexican or bittersweet
  chocolate, chopped

2 cinnamon sticks

½ cup Mexican crema

1. Spray the slow cooker with cooking spray. Add all the ingredients except the crema, stirring to blend.

2. Cook on low for 8 hours or on high for 4 hours, until the rice is soft and any liquid has thickened.

3. Remove the cinnamon sticks from the slow cooker and spoon the pudding into serving bowls and top with 1 or 2 tablespoons of crema per serving.

Ingredient Tip: Crema, or Mexican table cream, is like a tangier, slightly salty sour cream. It is unbelievably good on top of intense desserts like this rice pudding because it helps balance out the sweetness.

PINEAPPLE AND MANGO CRISP

Postre Crujiente de Piña y Mango

SERVES 6 • PREP TIME: 5 MINUTES • COOK TIME: 5 HOURS (LOW), 2½ HOURS (HIGH)

Tropical flavors abound in this fresh dessert that is perfect anytime of the year. Pineapple and mango combine with dark rum and candied ginger to entice you to take just one more bite. It's even quicker and easier if you buy pineapple and mango that is already peeled and cut. You'll only need to mix it up and sprinkle on the granola. Cooking doesn't get much easier than this. Other fruit combinations work just as well. Try peach and raspberry; strawberry and rhubarb; or blackberry, blueberry, and raspberry when these fruits are in season.

4 tablespoons unsalted butter, cut into tiny pieces, plus more for greasing the slow cooker

3 cups diced pineapple, drained if canned

2 cups diced mango

½ cup packed brown sugar

¼ cup orange or pineapple juice

2 tablespoons dark rum

¼ cup chopped candied ginger (optional)

2½ cups granola

1. Generously grease the slow cooker with butter.

2. In the slow cooker, combine all the ingredients except the granola and remaining 4 tablespoons of butter.

3. Scatter the butter pieces on top of the fruit, and sprinkle the granola on top of the butter.

4. Cook on low for 5 hours or on high for 2½ hours, until the fruit is tender.

5. Serve hot.

TEQUILA-POACHED PEARS

Peras al Tequila

SERVES 6 · PREP TIME: 15 MINUTES · COOK TIME: 6 HOURS (LOW), 3 HOURS (HIGH)

Poached pears are an elegant classic, and when given a Mexican twist, they are unexpected and fun. The tequila kicks up the flavor a little without being overpowering. This is also a beautiful dessert when served with a swirl of blush-colored prickly pear syrup and a scoop of lime sherbet or sorbet. Although any pears will do in this recipe, red Anjous seem to hold their shape and have more flavor than other varieties. If you have trouble getting your pears to stand upright in the slow cooker, trim a little off the bottom to make flatter, more stable bases.

6 Anjou pears, peeled

2 cups water

1½ cups sugar

2 cups pear nectar

1 cup tequila

2 tablespoons fresh lime juice

Zest from 1 lime

Prickly pear syrup (optional)

Lime sherbet or sorbet (optional)

1. Using a melon baller, remove the cores from the pears from the bottom.

2. In a medium saucepan over medium-high heat, combine the remaining ingredients except the syrup and sherbet and bring the mixture to a boil, stirring often. Boil for 1 minute.

3. In the slow cooker, place the pears stem-side up, pour the boiling liquid over the pears, and cook on low for 6 hours or on high for 3 hours, until the pears are tender but still hold their shape.

4. Drizzle a little prickly pear syrup, if using, on each dessert plate. Top with a poached pear and a scoop of lime sherbet, if using, and serve warm or cold.

TRES LECHES BREAD PUDDING

Budín de Pan Estilo Tres Leches

SERVES 6 • PREP TIME; 5 MINUTES • COOK TIME: 4 HOURS (LOW)

Tres leches *cake is a popular Mexican dessert, often served on special occasions. It consists of a butter cake soaked in sweetened condensed, evaporated, and whole milk—thus the name* tres leches *(three milks). This bread pudding is a twist on that beloved sweet. The third milk in this recipe is nondairy coconut milk, which lightens it a little while giving a delicate coconut flavor to the dessert. Since it cooks slowly, the custard becomes very silky, making this old-fashioned bread pudding very sophisticated. Serve this warm with a dollop of lightly sweetened whipped cream and watch the entire batch disappear in minutes.*

Cooking spray

1 (14-ounce) can sweetened condensed milk

1 (12-ounce) can evaporated milk

1 cup vanilla-flavored coconut milk

2 tablespoons dark rum (optional)

1 teaspoon ground cinnamon

6 egg yolks

1 (12-ounce) loaf French bread, cut into cubes

1. Spray the slow cooker with cooking spray.

2. In a large bowl, whisk together all the ingredients except the bread.

3. Add the cubed bread to the milk mixture and stir well to combine.

4. In the slow cooker, add the mixture and cook on low for 4 hours, or until the center of the pudding is set.

5. Serve warm.

Ingredient Variation: For a delicious variation on this recipe, cut 8 ounces of cream cheese into cubes and stir it into the custard base with the bread cubes. The tangy cream cheese is a nice contrast to the sweetness. It's almost like finding little pieces of cheesecake in your pudding.

10

KITCHEN STAPLES

~~~~~~~~~~~~~~~~~~

One thing that is consistent about good, authentic Mexican food is that the ingredients are always fresh. Sauces are simmered for long hours on the stove and not poured from a can. Seasonings are ground up just before use in the molecajete, tortillas are made daily, and vegetables and fruits come from local sources. Meals are not hurried but enjoyed.

Here you'll find instructions for making a few of the foundational foods of Mexican cooking. These recipes are not necessarily quick and easy, nor are they or meant for the slow cooker. If you want the most flavorful Mexican food, you'll need to prepare homemade sauces and work with fresh ingredients. Although these recipes take more effort than the slow-cooker recipes do, you can make them ahead of time. Many of these items freeze well, which is noted in the recipe headings. Many of them can also be made in bulk and kept in storage in the refrigerator or pantry.

CORN TORTILLAS

Tortillas de Maíz

MAKES 18 TORTILLAS · PREP TIME: 20 MINUTES, PLUS RESTING TIME
COOK TIME: 20 MINUTES

Corn tortillas are the foundation of Mexican food. If you've never had a fresh tortilla, you really haven't tasted tortillas at all. There is a learning curve to these—once you've made them several times, it is almost as quick to make them as it is to go to the store and buy them. It's a good idea to make a lot at once, since they freeze well.

If you are going to make tortillas often, do invest in a tortilla press and a comal. Neither is very expensive, and they will make the process much quicker and easier. When using these tools, your tortillas will be consistent in size and shape. You will realize just how important this is if you ever try to make a taco with a tortilla shaped like Kentucky.

2 cups plus 2 tablespoons masa harina

1½ cups hot water

Pinch sea salt (optional)

1. In a large bowl, mix together the masa harina, hot water, and salt until thoroughly combined.

2. Turn the dough out onto a clean, smooth surface and knead it until it is smooth and pliable. Don't let it dry out. If it's too sticky, add a little more masa harina. Continue to knead the dough for 3 minutes after it becomes pliable, and then form it into a ball. Cover the dough tightly with plastic wrap and let it rest for 1 hour at room temperature.

3. Preheat a comal, heavy cast iron skillet, or heavy stainless steel skillet over medium-high heat. While the pan is heating, cut 36 parchment circles the size of the tortilla press.

4. Divide the rested dough into 18 golf ball-size pieces. Place one parchment circle on the tortilla press and add a ball of dough. Top with another circle of parchment and press down on the top of the tortilla press to flatten the dough.

5. Immediately remove the top circle of parchment and transfer the tortilla top-side down onto the comal or skillet. Remove the bottom piece of parchment. Cook for 30 seconds, or until the tortilla is browned and a little puffy. Flip the tortilla and brown for 30 seconds more. Transfer the cooked tortilla to a plate and repeat with the remaining dough.

6. Keep the tortillas covered with a warm, damp towel until it's time to serve them.

Cooking Tip: Flip the tortilla when it no longer sticks to the comal. Pressing down gently on the middle of the tortilla as it cooks helps it puff up from the steam trapped inside. Tortillas that puff are more tender (they will deflate within seconds—that's normal). If they won't puff, turn them over one more time and gently press down on the center.

FLOUR TORTILLAS

Tortillas de Harina

MAKES 12 TORTILLAS ◦ PREP TIME: 10 MINUTES, PLUS RESTING TIME ◦
COOK TIME: 25 MINUTES

*While corn is indigenous to Mexico, flour and flour tortillas have been around only since
Spanish settlers began importing wheat. Flour tortillas are easy to make. Just be sure
to let the dough rest long enough, or the tortillas will be tough. A tortilla press will make
them too thick; if you use a press, roll out the tortillas by hand to thin them. Tortillas can
be stacked with parchment paper squares in between and frozen in airtight freezer bags
for up to 3 months.*

4 cups all-purpose flour

2 teaspoons baking powder

1 teaspoon sea salt

2 tablespoons lard

1½ cups hot water

*Ingredient Variation: Whole-wheat tortillas have a hearty, nutty flavor that stands up to
the spices and sauces in Mexican cooking. You can use this recipe to make whole-wheat
tortillas—just swap in these ingredients:*

4 cups whole-wheat flour
   (Montana white wheat flour is best)

1 teaspoon sea salt

½ cup olive oil, lard, or shortening

1 cup water

1. In a large bowl, whisk together the flour, baking powder, and salt.

2. Mix in the lard with your fingers until the flour is pebbly. Add the water and
   stir with a wooden spoon until the dough comes together in a ball.

3. Place the dough on a lightly floured surface and knead it until it is smooth
   and elastic.

4. Divide the dough into 12 pieces and cover them with a damp towel. Let the
   dough rest at room temperature for 30 minutes.

5. Preheat a comal or heavy skillet over medium-high heat.

6. Roll the dough out into thin circles with a floured rolling pin on a lightly floured surface.

7. Place a circle of dough on the hot comal until it is browned on one side. Flip the tortilla and cook it for another 1 to 2 minutes until the other side is browned. Press gently on the middle of the tortilla while it is cooking to make it puff. Repeat with the remaining dough.

8. Keep the cooked tortillas wrapped in a warm, moist towel until you are ready to use them.

GUACAMOLE

SERVES 6 · PREP TIME: 10 MINUTES, PLUS RESTING TIME

❦ *It's important to use ripe avocados for guacamole; they should feel firm but give a little when you squeeze gently. To speed ripening, place them in a closed paper bag at room temperature.*

The lime keeps the avocado flesh from oxidizing and turning an unappetizing shade of brown. You might or might not need both limes in this recipe—it depends on the size of the avocados and limes that you use. Guacamole is an ideal condiment for tacos, tostadas, fajitas, or nachos, or serve it with tortilla chips for a great snack.

3 Haas avocados, halved and pitted

2 limes, halved

½ teaspoon sea salt

½ medium onion, chopped

1 jalapeño, seeded and minced

2 Roma tomatoes, chopped

2 tablespoons chopped fresh cilantro

1 garlic clove, minced

1. Into a large bowl, scoop out the flesh of the avocado halves and squeeze the lime halves over the avocado; toss to coat completely.

2. Add the salt to the bowl and mash it into the avocado with a fork.

3. Gently stir in the onion, jalapeño, tomatoes, cilantro, and garlic.

4. Cover the bowl with plastic wrap and let it rest for 1 hour at room temperature.

5. Taste for seasonings, add more lime if necessary, and serve.

Ingredient Tip: Do not put whole avocados in the refrigerator unless you want to slow down the ripening process. They need to be at room temperature to ripen properly.

POBLANO MOLE

Mole Poblano

MAKES 12 CUPS CONCENTRATED MOLE · PREP TIME: 1 HOUR ·
COOK TIME: 30 MINUTES (STOVE TOP) PLUS 2 TO 4 HOURS (LOW)

❦❦❦ *According to legend, mole originated in the city of Puebla during the sixteenth century. Nuns from the Convent of Santa Rosa learned that the archbishop was to visit them. They panicked, because theirs was a poor convent and they had nothing to serve him. They prayed desperately for an answer, and an angel came, bringing them inspiration. They began grinding, roasting, and chopping everything they could find, including a crust of stale bread and a bit of chocolate. They used more than 20 ingredients. This mixture, which was cooked for hours until it reduced to a thick, dark sauce, was the first mole. The nuns served it with some old turkey, so the story goes, and the dish delighted the archbishop. With that, the national dish of Mexico was born.*

Although the ingredient list is long, the sauce is not hard to make. Once you try this, you will become very critical of the moles you get at restaurants or out of jars. This sauce has many complex layers of flavor and heat. The recipe makes a lot, but it will keep in the refrigerator for up to a month and in your freezer for up to a year. Use it for enchiladas or as a cooking sauce for any meat.

1 medium onion, chopped

6 dried ancho chiles, stemmed and seeded (seeds reserved)

15 dried pasilla chiles, stemmed and seeded (seeds reserved)

6 dried mulato chiles, stemmed and seeded (seeds reserved)

4 dried chipotles chiles, stemmed and seeded (seeds reserved)

15 dried guajillo chiles, stemmed and seeded (seeds reserved)

½ cup olive oil

6 garlic cloves, finely chopped

3 tablespoons raw almonds with skin

2 tablespoons raw shelled peanuts

3 tablespoons raisins

1 tablespoon pepitas (pumpkin seeds)

4 tablespoons sesame seeds

5 whole cloves

¼ teaspoon aniseed

¼ teaspoon coriander seeds

½ teaspoon peppercorns

1 teaspoon ground roasted cinnamon

¼ teaspoon ground allspice

2 ounces thickly sliced stale baguette

½ pound Roma tomatoes, fire-roasted

⅓ pound husked tomatillos, fire-roasted

6 ounces Mexican chocolate

5 cups Chicken Stock (see page 46)

Continued

1. In a large, heavy cast iron frying pan over medium-high heat, heat the olive oil until it is very hot but not smoking, about 2 minutes. Add about half of the chiles to the pan and toast them for 1 to 2 minutes, stirring constantly.

2. Using a slotted spoon, remove that batch to a bowl and repeat with the rest. Don't overcrowd the skillet. If your skillet is too small, toast them in three batches.

3. Add the onion and garlic to the same oil in the skillet. Sauté for 2 or 3 minutes over medium-high heat, stirring constantly, until the vegetables soften. Add the almonds, peanuts, raisins, and pepitas. Cook, stirring for 3 minutes. Stir in the sesame seeds, reserved chile seeds, cloves, aniseeds, coriander, peppercorns, cinnamon, and allspice. Cook, stirring constantly, for 4 minutes.

4. In the slow cooker, combine the contents of the pan, the bread, tomatoes, tomatillos, chiles, chocolate, and chicken stock, and cook on low for 2 to 4 hours, or until the flavors have melded.

5. In a blender, purée the mixture in batches. Use immediately or refrigerate or freeze for future use. When you're ready to use the frozen mole again, set a stockpot on the stove over medium-high heat. Add ½ cup stock to 1 cup of mole and simmer for 5 minutes before serving.

Ingredient Variation: You can easily make this vegan by substituting Vegetable Stock (see page 48) for the chicken stock in this recipe. Add the mole to sautéed mushrooms, veggie burgers, or cooked beans. Try slow-cooking cubed eggplant in this sauce sometime. It's incredible.

PICO DE GALLO

MAKES 2½ TO 3 CUPS • PREP TIME: 10 MINUTES

Pico de gallo, *which literally means "rooster's beak," is a salsa commonly served in Mexico, where it is also called* salsa Mexicana *or* salsa picada. *It is more like a relish than the salsas that Americans are used to. Because the ingredients are so fresh, this condiment brings a fresh, summery flavor to everything you spoon it on, from tacos to fajitas.*

For the best flavor, use fully ripe tomatoes. This is not a recipe you will be able to make successfully when tomatoes are out of season. The ingredients can be coarsely chopped and chunky, or you can pulse them briefly in a food processor for a more finely chopped version.

Pico de Gallo will keep for several days in a tightly closed container in the refrigerator but does not freeze well.

6 Roma tomatoes, diced

3 jalapeños, seeded and chopped

3 scallions, chopped

1 onion, chopped

1 garlic clove, chopped

½ bunch fresh cilantro, chopped

Pinch of sea salt

2 limes

1. In a large bowl, combine all the ingredients except the limes.

2. Squeeze the juice of one lime into the bowl. Stir gently and let stand for 15 minutes.

3. Taste and add salt and more lime as needed before serving.

ALL ABOUT TOMATILLOS

Tomatillos originated in Mexico and are an important part of Mexican cuisine. The fruit has an inedible dry husk around it. As the fruit matures, it fills the husk, and eventually the husk splits open. This husk must be removed before using the tomatillo, but it is easily pulled off and discarded. The fruit should then be rinsed to remove any of the sticky, sappy substance from the husk.

Choose smallish fruit that are fresh looking and bright green with husks that look fresh and not too shriveled. The fruit should be firm to the touch without bruises or defects.

Leave the husks intact for storage, removing them only when you are ready to use the tomatillos. You can store them on the counter or in the refrigerator. They'll keep for up to a month and can be frozen whole for longer storage.

Don't peel the green skin or remove the seeds. Once your tomatillos are husked and rinsed, they are ready to be used in any recipe.

GREEN SALSA

Salsa Verde

MAKES 2 CUPS * PREP TIME: 20 MINUTES * COOK TIME: 15 MINUTES

❦❦❦ Tomatillos give this green salsa a zesty flavor that is especially delicious on poultry and fish. This homemade version is so quick to make that there is no reason to eat any other kind. The main difference between green and red salsas is the use of tomatillos instead of tomatoes. In a traditional green salsa, you won't find oregano, cumin, or lime, but they make for a flavorful twist on the original.

Green salsa was originally made with a molcajete, but modern cooks prefer the food processor or blender. If you don't have a food processor or blender, you can make this by chopping the ingredients and then adding a cup of water when you cook it. Keep an eye on it and stir it often, adding more water as needed. This salsa freezes well.

1 pound husked tomatillos, chopped

½ medium onion, chopped

3 garlic cloves, chopped

2 serrano chiles, seeded and chopped

1 poblano chile, fire-roasted, skinned, seeded, and chopped (see page 158)

1 teaspoon dried Mexican oregano

½ teaspoon ground cumin

½ cup chopped fresh cilantro

Juice of ½ lime

½ teaspoon sea salt

1. In a food processor, pulse the tomatillos, onion, garlic, serrano chiles, and poblano chile into chunks, until the mixture resembles a coarse sauce.

2. In a medium saucepan over medium heat, add the chile mixture, oregano, and cumin. Simmer while stirring often, for about 15 minutes, adding a little water if the salsa becomes too thick.

3. Pour the salsa into a serving bowl and stir in the cilantro, lime juice, and salt. Taste and adjust the seasonings as necessary.

PICKLED VEGETABLES

Verduras en Escabeche

SERVES 6 TO 8 · PREP TIME: 20 MINUTES · COOK TIME: 15 MINUTES, PLUS OVERNIGHT

❦ *Many restaurants in Mexico serve pickled vegetables rather than chips and salsa. The dish is related to the Italian* giardiniera, *a mixture of seasonal vegetables pickled in vinegar. Pickling is relatively new in Mexico. Prior to the arrival of Europeans, Mexicans were not aware of the existence of vinegar, which is a by-product of winemaking.*

In Mexico pickled vegetables are usually made with white (distilled) vinegar, sometimes in combination with red wine or sherry vinegar. Apple cider vinegar is widely available, so it is used here, but if you have pineapple vinegar, use it instead.

These tangy, crispy vegetables have a little heat to them, which tends to increase the longer they stand. If you want them spicier, add more jalapeños or add a hot dried chile to the storage container.

¾ cup olive oil

12 garlic cloves

1 onion, cut into wedges

4 carrots, sliced diagonally

2 teaspoons whole allspice

1 teaspoon peppercorns

1 teaspoon dried thyme

1 teaspoon dried Mexican oregano

1 teaspoon dried marjoram

8 bay leaves

Sea salt

1 head cauliflower, cored and cut into florets

4 jalapeños, seeded and chopped

1½ cups apple cider vinegar

1 cup water

3 zucchini, sliced diagonally

1 (1-pound) jicama, peeled and diced

1. In a heavy pot over medium heat, heat the olive oil. When the oil is very hot but not smoking, add the garlic and onion. Sauté for 3 minutes, stirring constantly, then lower the heat to medium-low.

2. Add the carrots, allspice, peppercorns, thyme, oregano, marjoram, and bay leaves. Cover and cook for 2 minutes. Taste and season with salt as needed.

3. Add the cauliflower, jalapeños, vinegar, and water. Stir and cover the pot. Cook for 4 minutes.

4. Add the zucchini and jicama to the pot. Cook for 4 more minutes. Do not overcook—the vegetables should still have crunch.

5. Remove the pot from the heat and discard the bay leaves. Place the vegetables and their liquid in an airtight container and refrigerate overnight.

6. Serve the pickles at room temperature.

Cooking Tip: Always use glass or other nonreactive bowls, enamel pots, wooden cooking utensils, and glass or plastic storage containers when working with vinegar. Aluminum and other reactive metals will discolor and add an odd flavor to the pickles. Copper, brass, iron, and galvanized utensils should never be used.

TACO SEASONING MIX

Sazonador para Tacos Tex-Mex

MAKES 3 TABLESPOONS · PREP TIME: 5 MINUTES

Confession time: Taco seasoning mix is not native to Mexico. However, taco season-ing is fantastic to have on hand to make Tex-Mex-style tacos, season meat and poultry, and sprinkle on homemade tortilla chips. This recipe beats the commercial mixes by a long shot.

Most taco seasonings have chili powder in them. Chili powder is not a spice; it is a combination of spices that include cumin. Different brands of chili powder have different amounts of cumin. Keep that in mind when you are mixing things up.

You can make this seasoning in large amounts and store it in an airtight plastic con-tainer in the pantry.

1 tablespoon chili powder

1 teaspoon packed brown sugar

½ teaspoon smoked paprika

½ teaspoon ground cumin, if needed

½ teaspoon smoked salt or sea salt

¼ teaspoon garlic powder

¼ teaspoon onion powder

¼ teaspoon chipotle powder

¼ teaspoon dried Mexican oregano

Pinch of cayenne pepper

Pinch of freshly ground black pepper

1. In an airtight container, combine all of the ingredients, and keep the mixture in a cool, dry pantry.

2. Use 3 tablespoons of seasoning per pound of meat.

FAJITA SEASONING MIX

Sazonador para Fajitas

MAKES 3 TABLESPOONS • PREP TIME: 5 MINUTES

Fajita seasoning is another basic seasoning mix that is easy and inexpensive to make. Like taco seasoning, it has a variety of uses besides fajitas. You can sprinkle it on salads, season roasted and grilled meats with it, and add it to melted butter to be brushed on potatoes before roasting. The possibilities are endless.

Find a store that sells herbs and spices in bulk, such as Whole Foods or Sprouts. Buying spices in bulk saves money, and bulk spices are usually much fresher than those sold in jars. Also, you can buy large amounts and make this spice mixture up by the gallon if you want to. It stores perfectly in a cool, dark pantry.

1 tablespoon cornstarch

2 teaspoons chili powder

1 teaspoon lime zest powder (may omit or use a pinch of fresh lime zest)

1 teaspoon sea salt

1 teaspoon smoked paprika

1 teaspoon sugar

½ teaspoon crushed chicken bouillon cube

½ teaspoon onion powder

¼ teaspoon freshly ground black pepper

¼ teaspoon cayenne pepper

¼ teaspoon ground cumin

¼ teaspoon garlic powder

1. In an airtight container, combine all of the ingredients and keep the mixture in a cool, dry pantry.

2. Use 3 tablespoons of seasoning per pound of meat.

FIRE-ROASTED CHILES AND VEGETABLES

Chiles y Verduras Asadas

Fire-roasted chiles, peppers, tomatoes, tomatillos, and other vegetables give a distinctive smoky flavor to Mexican foods. Even if your recipe doesn't call for fire-roasted (a nice name for blackened) ingredients, you can usually add another layer of flavor by spending a few minutes blackening them before using.

Fire-roasting is easy and can be done under the broiler, on the grill, on a gas stove, or with a propane torch. The trick is to make sure that the heat is extremely high—let the broiler or stove preheat for at least 5 minutes, and let the grill preheat for at least 10 minutes. If the temperature is too cool when you start to roast, your ingredients will cook before they blacken.

Tomatoes, tomatillos, chiles, and bell peppers can be roasted whole. Onions should be cut into chunks before roasting.

To grill

1. Preheat the grill on high for at least 10 minutes.
2. Brush the grill grate with olive oil.
3. Place the whole vegetable on the grate.
4. Watch carefully and turn the vegetable often with tongs until it is blackened on all sides.

To use a propane torch

1. Light the torch.
2. Pick up the chile or other vegetable with fireproof tongs.
3. Move the tongs so that the vegetable is moving up and down the fire until the skin blisters and it blackens on all sides.
4. Alternatively, you can place the vegetable on a heatproof surface and move the torch.

To use the broiler

1. Move the oven rack to within 4 inches of the heating element in the broiler.

2. Preheat the broiler on high for at least 5 minutes until it is very hot.

3. Place whole vegetables on a heavy baking sheet under the broiler.

4. Broil the vegetables, turning them often with tongs, until they have blackened on all sides. Watch carefully, because once they begin to blacken, they can burn quickly.

5. Most vegetables will take about 10 to 15 minutes to blacken completely under the broiler.

To use the gas stove

1. Turn on the stove, setting the flame to high.

2. Hold the vegetable over the flame with fireproof tongs until it is charred on all sides.

Once the skins are blackened, no matter which method you use, place the vegetables in a heatproof bowl. Cover the top tightly with plastic wrap and leave them on the kitchen counter for 10 minutes. At the end of that time, the skins will slip right off and the vegetables will be ready to use. The tomatillo skins do not peel off—use the tomatillos as they are.

> **Warning:** When you are fire-roasting chiles, do it in a well-ventilated area. Keep the exhaust fan on if you are working inside. Do not breathe in any resulting smoke and don't get it in your eyes. The same chemicals in the chiles that will burn your fingers will irritate your throat, lungs, and eyes, too.

THE DIRTY DOZEN & CLEAN FIFTEEN

A nonprofit and environmental watchdog organization called Environmental Working Group (EWG) looks at data supplied by the US Department of Agriculture (USDA) and the Food and Drug Administration (FDA) about pesticide residues and compiles a list each year of the best and worst pesticide loads found in commercial crops. You can use these lists to decide which fruits and vegetables to buy organic to minimize your exposure to pesticides and which produce is considered safe enough to skip the organics. This does not mean they are pesticide-free, though, so wash these fruits and vegetables thoroughly.

These lists change every year, so make sure you look up the most recent before you fill your shopping cart. You'll find the most recent lists as well as a guide to pesticides in produce at EWG.org/FoodNews.

2015 DIRTY DOZEN

Apples	Peaches
Celery	Potatoes
Cherry tomatoes	Snap peas (imported)
Cucumbers	Spinach
Grapes	Strawberries
Nectarines (imported)	Sweet bell peppers

In addition to the dirty dozen, the EWG added three produce contaminated with highly toxic organophosphate insecticides:

Collard greens	Hot peppers
Kale	

2015 CLEAN FIFTEEN

Asparagus	Mangoes
Avocados	Onions
Cabbage	Papayas
Cantaloupes	Pineapples
Cauliflower	Sweet corn
Eggplants	Sweet peas (frozen)
Grapefruits	Sweet potatoes
Kiwis	

APPENDIX B
MEASUREMENT CONVERSIONS

VOLUME EQUIVALENTS (LIQUID)

US STANDARD	US STANDARD (OUNCES)	METRIC (APPROXIMATE)
2 tablespoons	1 fl. oz.	30 mL
¼ cup	2 fl. oz.	60 mL
½ cup	4 fl. oz.	120 mL
1 cup	8 fl. oz.	240 mL
1½ cups	12 fl. oz.	355 mL
2 cups or 1 pint	16 fl. oz.	475 mL
4 cups or 1 quart	32 fl. oz.	1 L
1 gallon	128 fl. oz.	4 L

OVEN TEMPERATURES

FAHRENHEIT (F)	CELSIUS (C) (APPROXIMATE)
250°	120°
300°	150°
325°	165°
350°	180°
375°	190°
400°	200°
425°	220°
450°	230°

VOLUME EQUIVALENTS (DRY)

US STANDARD	METRIC (APPROXIMATE)
⅛ teaspoon	0.5 mL
¼ teaspoon	1 mL
½ teaspoon	2 mL
¾ teaspoon	4 mL
1 teaspoon	5 mL
1 tablespoon	15 mL
¼ cup	59 mL
⅓ cup	79 mL
½ cup	118 mL
⅔ cup	156 mL
¾ cup	177 mL
1 cup	235 mL
2 cups or 1 pint	475 mL
3 cups	700 mL
4 cups or 1 quart	1 L

WEIGHT EQUIVALENTS

US STANDARD	METRIC (APPROXIMATE)
½ ounce	15 g
1 ounce	30 g
2 ounces	60 g
4 ounces	115 g
8 ounces	225 g
12 ounces	340 g
16 ounces or 1 pound	455 g

INGREDIENTS GLOSSARY

Adobo: A spicy sauce used to marinate foods and to cook meat.

Arborio: A medium-grained rice that gets creamy and chewy when cooked. It's often used for rice pudding.

Cajeta: A thick sauce, somewhat like caramel sauce, made from cooking sweetened goat's milk for a long time. It's tangier than caramel.

Calabacitas: A summer squash very much like zucchini. Zucchini can be substituted.

Cilantro: An herb, usually used fresh, that has a warm, earthy flavor. It is used both for flavor and for garnishing foods.

Crema: A thick cream that is tangy and slightly salty—similar to crème fraîche or sour cream. It can be found jarred in the dairy section or canned in the Mexican food section of many grocery stores.

Dulce de leche: A thick sauce, somewhat like caramel, that is made from cooking sweetened cow's milk for a long time. Sweeter than *cajeta*.

Fire-roasting: Blackening the outer skin of a vegetable by grilling, broiling, or other methods. It's generally done with tomatoes, chiles, onions, and tomatillos.

Hominy: Kernels of field corn that are soaked in limewater that removes the hull of the corn and causes the grain to puff up.

Masa harina: A type of flour made with nixtamalized corn (soaked, cooked in lime water, and hulled) that has been dried and ground. It is used to make corn tortillas, tamales, and other Mexican snacks.

Mexican chocolate: A grainy chocolate flavored with cinnamon, almonds, and vanilla. To substitute bittersweet chocolate, add ½ teaspoon cinnamon and 1 drop almond extract per ounce.

Mexican oregano: An herb that tastes similar to Mediterranean oregano but is earthier and has a citrus flavor. It is a totally different plant.

Roasted cinnamon: Cinnamon that has been roasted and ground. Roasting brings out the sweetness of the spice. Regular ground cinnamon can be substituted.

REFERENCES

Breast Cancer Fund. "Tips for Avoiding BPA in Canned Food." Accessed August 8, 2015. www.breastcancerfund.org/reduce-your -risk/tips/avoid-bpa.html.

Friesen, Katy June. "Where Did the Taco Come From?" Smithsonian.com. Accessed August 8, 2015. www.smithsonianmag.com /arts-culture/where-did-the-taco-come -from-81228162/?no-ist.

Gorman, Rachel Moeller. "Fresh vs. Frozen Vegetables: Are We Giving up Nutrition for Convenience?" *Eating Well.* Accessed August 8, 2015. www.eatingwell.com /nutrition_health/nutrition_news _information/fresh_vs_frozen_vegetables _are_we_giving_up_nutrition_fo.

Gourmet Sleuth. "Enchiladas." Accessed August 8, 2015. www.gourmetsleuth.com /articles/detail/enchiladas.

Schneider, Deborah. *The Mexican Slow Cooker: Recipes for Mole, Enchiladas, Carnitas, Chile Verde Pork, and More Favorites.* Berkeley, CA: Ten Speed Press, 2012.

Spanish Language Stack Exchange. "Where Did Pico de Gallo Get Its Name?" Accessed August 8, 2015. spanish.stackexchange.com/questions /1325/where-did-pico-de-gallo-get -its-name.

Specialty Produce. "Chayote Squash." Accessed August 8, 2015. www.specialtyproduce.com/produce /Chayote_Squash_538.php#sthash .WTrRRk1l.dpuf.

World Food Wine. "Mexican Food History." Accessed August 8, 2015. world-food-and -wine.com/mexican-food-history.

RECIPE INDEX

INDEX

Index

ABOUT THE AUTHOR

MARYE AUDET is a food writer and recipe developer who lives in North Texas. Her recipes can be found online at www.restlesschipotle.com. When not writing, she can often be found with a mango margarita in one hand and a bowl of pozole in the other.

CPSIA information can be obtained at www.ICGtesting.com
Printed in the USA
BVOW07s1430251115

428502BV00025B/152/P